Hannes Gumtau
Wolfgang Kurschatke

Englische Grammatik für den Realschulabschluss üben

8.–10. Schuljahr

Lena Stahlmann

MANZ VERLAG

5. Auflage 2007
Manz Verlag

Lektorat: Harald Kotlarz, Rottenburg
Herstellung: Karin Schmid, Baldham
Illustrationen: Sven Palmowski, El Prat de Llobregat
Umschlagkonzept: KünkelLopka, Heidelberg
Umschlagfoto: Fotostudio Maurer, Bamberg
Druck: Finidr s.r.o., Český Těšín

ISBN: 978-3-7863-2018-0

www.manz-verlag.de

Liebe Schülerin, lieber Schüler,

Wozu diese Lernhilfe?

Um englische Grammatik zu üben und sicher zu beherrschen, wenn es darauf ankommt.

Welche Grammatik?

Einfach alles, was immer wieder verlangt wird und wo sich erfahrungsgemäß Fehler einschleichen können.

Welches Ziel steckt dahinter?

Dich fit in englischer Grammatik zu machen, damit du in schriftlichen Arbeiten und in der Realschulabschlussprüfung keine Fehler machst (oder fast keine). Bestimmt hast du schon gemerkt, dass die Beherrschung der Grammatik für jede Art von Fragestellung in der Prüfung wichtig ist.

Wie solltest du vorgehen?

In drei Schritten zum Ziel:

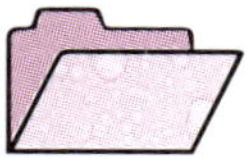

1. Du wiederholst das Grundwissen.
In jeder Übung kannst du einen Aspekt einer grammatischen Form wiederholen.

Blickst du mal nicht durch, dann helfen dir die *tipps & tricks* weiter

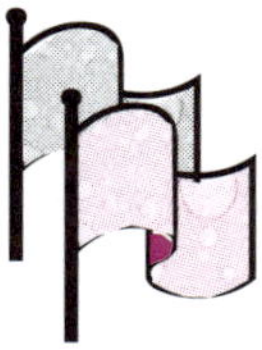

2. Du wendest das Grundwissen an.
Im ersten Schritt hast du die Formen einzeln geübt, hier kommen sie alle zusammen vor, so wie auch in schriftlichen Arbeiten und beim Sprechen.

3. Du bearbeitest Prüfungsaufgaben.
Hier kannst du sehen, in welchen Aufgabentypen Grammatik vorkommt. Ob *guided writing* oder *vocabulary*, überall findest du „versteckte" Grammatikfragen.

Wenn du dieses Bild siehst, musst du Fehler selbst erkennen und korrigieren.

Lösungen zu allen Übungen findest du im hinteren Teil des Buches.

Alles klar? Dann kann's losgehen.

Viele Spaß und Erfolg dabei!

Inhalt

A Mengenbezeichnungen

Some und *any*

1. Look at the picture and then put in **some** or **any**.

a) Are there ____________ lions on the farm? – No I can't see ____________; but I can see ____________ hens.

b) Are there ____________ horses on the farm? – Yes, there are. There are ____________ cows, too.

c) There's ____________ tea in the pot, but we haven't got ____________ sugar.

d) Have you ____________ idea when the performance begins?

e) You can't have ____________ more meat; we must save ____________ for your brother.

f) Can I have ____________ more tea, please? – Yes, of course.

2. Say it in English.

a) Frage Tom, ob er noch etwas Milch möchte.

____?

b) Sage, dass du noch etwas Tee haben möchtest, aber ohne Zucker.

____?

c) Sage, dass Tom auf der Farm Hühner, aber keine Gänse gesehen hat.

____?

d) Frage Judy, ob sie in der Stadt Bücher oder CDs gekauft hat.

____?

Du verwendest ***some*** vor allem in bejahten Aussagesätzen und ***any*** vor allem in verneinten Aussagesätzen und Fragen. ***Some*** steht auch in Fragen, die eine höfliche Bitte oder ein Angebot ausdrücken.

Zusammensetzungen mit *some* und *any*

3. Something or anything? Someone or anyone? Somewhere or anywhere?

a) There was a noise outside. I heard __________________ in the garden.

b) Did you see my hat __________________? – No, I didn't see it __________________.

c) Shall we tell you __________________ very interesting? I don't want to hear __________________. I am too tired.

d) Look. There's __________________ in the car. It's a suitcase. Can you see __________________ in it? – No, I can't see __________________.

e) John is hungry. He wants __________________ to eat, but he doesn't want __________________ to drink.

f) Is there ______________ in the fridge? I'm hungry. – I'm sorry, there isn't ______________ left. But I can go and get ______________ at the supermarket.

g) Has ______________ seen the dog? It must be ______________ in the garden.

h) Susan didn't enjoy the party because she didn't know ______________.

i) The doorbell is ringing. There must be ______________ at the door.

much – many – a lot of

4. Fill in **much, many** or **a lot of.**

a) How ____________ friends have you got? – I've got ____________ friends.

b) How ____________ sugar do you take in your tea? – I don't take ____________ because I don't like it too sweet.

c) How ____________ animals are there on the farm? – There aren't ____________, they are on the hills.

d) How ____________ money did Tom spend? – He didn't spend ____________, he was nearly broke.

e) How ____________ times did you visit London? – I was there ____________ times last year.

f) Tony got bad marks in his last test. There were ____________ mistakes in it.

Du nimmst ***much*** (= viel) bei nicht zählbaren Substantiven (z. B. *sugar*), ***many*** bei Substantiven im Plural (z. B. *animals*). Beide verwendest du meist in Fragen und verneinten Aussagesätzen. In bejahten Aussagesätzen nimmst du eher ***a lot of*** (= viele).

a little – a few

5. Fill in **a little** or **a few**.

a) There are only __________ potatoes left. We must go and buy some.

b) Robert is a good pupil. He only made __________ mistakes.

c) Diana only met __________ friends at the party. She was very disappointed.

d) The boys ate some sandwiches, but they only drank __________ of the alcohol.

e) There's __________ time left. We must hurry to catch the bus.

Bei nicht zählbaren Substantiven (z. B. *time*) nimmst du ***a little*** (= wenig), bei zählbaren (z. B. *potatoes*) nimmst du ***a few*** (= wenige).

each und *every*

6. Fill in **each** or **every**.

a) In the driving school there are tests __________ month.

b) __________ of the candidates had taken lessons before.

c) The lessons are £20 __________.

d) __________ time Lisa tried to start the car, it didn't go.

e) Fifty persons out of __________ hundred failed the test.

f) In __________ case the examiner had to take over the braking or steering.

g) __________ other day my friend practised driving.

Each heißt „jeder" von (aus einer bestimmten Anzahl), ***every*** bedeutet ganz allgemein „jeder".

7. **Say it in English.**

a) Sage, dass jeder in eurer Familie ein Auto hat.

____

b) Sage, dass man überall Fahrschulen finden kann.

____

c) Sage, dass es für einen Kandidaten unmöglich ist, alles zu wissen.

____

d) Sage, dass heute jeder etwas über Autos wissen muss.

____

Die **Zusammensetzungen** mit *every* heißen: ***everyone*** (= jeder), ***everything*** (= alles) und ***everywhere*** (= überall).

Vermischte Übungen

8. Fill in: **some – someone – something – somewhere – any – anyone – anything – anywhere – everyone – everything – everywhere**.

a) Is there ______________ in the garden? – No, there isn't ______________ in the garden. But there is ______________ in the house. I can hear ______________ singing a song.

b) Are there ______________ birds in the garden? – No, there aren't because there are ______________ cats on the lawn.

c) Is there ______________ red on the house? – Yes, I can see ______________ I think it's a bird.

d) Let's go down to the lake. We'll find a nice place ______________.

e) Which things are we going to take with us? We can't carry ______________.

f) We saw snack bars ______________ we went in America.

9. Say it in English.

a) Frage Jean wie viel Milch noch da ist.

____

b) Jean antwortet, dass noch viel Milch im Kühlschrank ist, aber nur ein wenig Apfelsaft.

____

____

c) Jean sagt, dass nur ein paar Zwiebeln da sind.

____

d) Du fragst, wie viele du kaufen sollst.

____

e) Jean sagt, dass du dich beeilen musst, weil nicht mehr viel Zeit bis zum Essen ist.

____

Prüfungsaufgaben

10. Answer the questions in complete sentences.

a) How many hours a week does Michael work for in total? (twenty) (2)

____

b) Why do some of the immigrant children have fewer language problems than others? (from India / English second language) (2)

____

____

11. Asking questions.

You would like to know the price of the ticket. (2)

____

12. Say it in English.

a) Mr Best will wissen, wie viel das neue Fremdsprachenprogramm kostet: (2)

____

b) Er bedankt sich herzlich: (2)

____

13. Translate into German.

a) Life has not changed in America over the last few decades. (2)

____

b) They don't earn enough money to pay for someone. (2)

____

c) But this will only be possible if they beat countries like ...,
some of whose players also play ... (3)

______________________________ ...

______________________________ ...

d) Each time the top event of the opening ceremony ... (2)

______________________________ ...

14. Underline the three mistakes and correct them. (3)

a) Every of the boys wants to play in the team. ______________

b) How many time have we left? ______________

c) I can tell you something very interesting. ______________

d) You must be very careful in each case. ______________

e) The doorbell is ringing. There must be anyone outside. ______________

B Pronomen

Personalpronomen – Possessivpronomen – Reflexivpronomen – reziprokes Pronomen – Relativpronomen

1. Fill in the missing pronouns.

a)	*I* open	*my* eyes.	Can you see	*me* ?
b)	*You* open	______ eyes.	I can see	______
c)	______ opens	______ eyes.	I can see	______
d)	______ opens	______ eyes.	I can see	______
e)	______ opens	______ eyes.	I can see	______
f)	______ open	______ eyes.	Can you see	______?
g)	______ open	______ eyes.	We can see	______
h)	______ open	______ eyes.	We can see	______

Unterscheide die Personalpronomen in der **Subjektform** (z. B. *I, you, he, she, it, we, you, they*) und die in der **Objektform** (z. B. *me, you, him, her it, us, you, them*). Die **adjektivisch gebrauchten** Possessivpronomen sind: *my, your, his, her, its, our, your, their.*

2. Replace the underlined words with pronouns.

a)	Tom gives Judy a book.	______ gives ______ a book.
b)	Kathryn and Peter invited me and my brother to their party.	______ invited ______ to their party.
c)	Gemma asked the policeman the way.	______ asked ______ the way.

d) Mr Brown invites his boss to his house. — __________ invites __________ to his house.

e) My brother and I gave the landlady some flowers. — __________ gave __________ some flowers.

f) Tony is selling his car next week. — __________ is selling __________ next week.

3. Fill in the correct possessive adjectives.

a) Judy has got a new dress. __________ colour is white.

b) Tom has got new inline skates. __________ hobby is skating.

c) Mrs Dawson says: "Judy you must do __________ homework first."

d) Mr and Mrs Dawson take __________ holidays in August.

e) Mr Dawson says: "Let's take __________ bikes with us."

f) Judy is taking __________ dog for a walk. __________ tail is wagging.

g) Mr Dawson: "You must clean __________ bikes, children. They are dirty."

h) Tom answers: "__________ bike isn't dirty. I cleaned it yesterday."

4. Fill in the correct pronouns.

a) This is Judy. __________ skirt is beautiful. __________ has fair hair.

b) Judy has a friend. __________ name is John. __________ is a nice boy.

c) __________ often go swimming at the weekends. __________ hobbies are swimming and dancing.

d) __________ best friends are Gordon and Mary. Gordon says to John: "__________ hobby is tennis, but __________ like __________ hobbies, too, John."

5. Fill in the missing possessive pronouns.

a) Give me the book. It's _________.

b) I give you the book. It's _________.

c) I give him the book. It's _________.

d) I give her the book. It's _________.

e) Give us the book. It's _________.

f) I give you the book. It's _________.

g) I give them the book. It's _________.

6. Fill in the correct pronouns.

a) Is this your father's car? Yes, it's _________.

b) This is not my book, Tony. It must be _________.

c) I've already invited all my friends. Has Judy invited _________?

d) Is this your game, children? No, it's not _________.

e) This can't be your CD Jane. I'm sure it's _________.

f) I've already done my homework. Have Tom and Judy done _________?

g) This isn't Peter's bike. _________ is old.

h) This isn't my ball. Is it _________,Tony?
Yes, it's _________.

Die **substantivisch** gebrauchten **Possessivpronomen** *(mine, yours, his, hers, its, ours, yours, theirs)* stehen allein, nicht bei einem Substantiv wie die adjektivisch gebrauchten *(my, your, …)*.

7. Put in the suitable reflexive pronoun.

a) We enjoyed ________________ at the party last Saturday.

b) The children hurt ________________ badly when skating.

c) The cat cut ________________ on some broken glass.

d) Jean, you must look after ________________.

e) Did you buy this new skirt, Judy? – No, I made it ________________.

f) Tom introduced ________________ when he met Mrs Brown for the first time.

g) Judy blamed ________________ for the mistakes she had made.

h) Look into this mirror, Tom and Judy. You can see ________________ there.

8. Translate.

a) Judy fragt Tom, wo sie sich treffen können.

____

b) Tom antwortet, dass er sich nicht an das Café in der Nähe des Bahnhofs erinnert.

____

c) Judy sagt, dass sich im letzten Jahr viel in der Stadt verändert hat.

____

d) Tom fragt, ob sie sich dem Jugendklub anschließen sollten.

____

e) Judy sagt, dass sich dort nicht viel ereignet.

____

f) Tom fragt sich, ob sie dort viele Freunde treffen werden.

____

Das **Reflexivpronomen** *(myself, yourself, himself, herself, itself, ourselves, yourselves, themselves)* wird rückbezüglich gebraucht oder es dient zur Hervorhebung eines Substantivs.
Beachte die Unterschiede: *to meet* = **sich** treffen

9. Fill in the correct reflexive or reciprocal pronoun where necessary.

a) Sabine and Tom looked at ________________ in the mirror, before they went to the party.

b) Sabine and Tom looked at ________________ surprised when they happened to meet.

c) Sabine has changed ________________ very much recently.

d) Sabine and Tom get along with ________________ very well.

e) Sabine will always remember ________________ her stay in England.

f) Sabine's friend is very practical. He repairs his car ________________.

Das reziproke Pronomen *(each other)* verwendest du, wenn du eine wechselseitige Beziehung (sich gegenseitig, einander) ausdrückst.

10. Say it in English.

Sage deinem Freund, dass

a) ihr euch lange nicht mehr gesehen habt.

____

b) du ihm nicht helfen kannst und dass er seine Hausaufgaben selbst machen muss.

____

____

c) du dich entschuldigst, wenn du zu spät kommst.

d) ihr euch auf der Party sehr amüsiert habt.

e) Tom und Mary sich im Kino getroffen haben.

11. Fill in: **who** or **which**.

a) I have a friend ____________ speaks excellent Japanese.

b) The letter ____________ arrived yesterday is from my aunt in Canada.

c) The film is about animals ____________ live in the jungle.

d) The boys ____________ painted the graffiti on the wall had to remove it.

e) The book is about a lady ____________ spent ten years in Africa.

f) Where can I find a shop ____________ sells T-shirts?

g) Sheila only eats food ____________ is grown in her own garden.

Du verwendest ***who*** für **Personen**, ***which*** für **Sachen** (und Tiere). Beide sind hier Subjekt eines Relativsatzes, z.B. *the girl who works* – das Mädchen, das arbeitet (Wer arbeitet?)

12. Fill in: **who** or **whose**.

a) Katie is the girl ____________ won first prize.

b) James is the boy ____________ parents have just moved here.

c) Debbie is the girl ____________ mother works in the school canteen.

d) Where is the house ____________ windows were broken?

e) Mrs Potter is the lady ___________ passed her driving test yesterday.

f) Is this the girl ___________ bike was stolen?

g) Where is the shop ___________ owner is your cousin?

Du bezeichnest mit ***whose*** eine **Zugehörigkeit** oder einen **Besitz**, z. B. *the shop whose owner* – der Laden, dessen Besitzer. Dagegen ist ***who*** hier Subjekt im Relativsatz, z. B. *the man who* – der Mann, der.

13. Fill in **who** or **which** if necessary.

a) The friends ___________ I have invited haven't come yet.

b) The window ___________ they broke has now been repaired.

c) David found the purse ___________ his sister had lost.

d) The car ___________ stopped in front of our house is a BMW.

e) The film ___________ we wanted to see was no longer showing.

f) Paul is the boy ___________ has invited us to his birthday party.

g) The music ___________ Rebecca likes best is by the Beatles.

h) Emma was the only girl ___________ spoke a little French.

i) Could you return the money ___________ I lent you last week?

Die Relativpronomen ***who*** bzw. ***which*** können **Subjekt** bzw. **Objekt** sein. Wenn sie als **Objekt** verwendet werden, fallen sie fast immer weg, also: *The money which I lent you.* ➧ *The money I lent you.* Vorsicht beim Übersetzen ins Deutsche! Hier erscheint das Relativpronomen wieder: Das Geld, **das** ich dir geliehen habe.

14. Put the preposition at the end of the relative clause and drop the relative pronoun.

a) John visited the town in which he was brought up.

b) The girl to whom you spoke is from form 9C.

c) This is the bus on which we came.

d) The country to which you are pointing is Ireland.

e) Is this the book in which you are interested?

f) The tourists to whom Emma was talking were from India.

g) India is a country about which I don't know very much.

h) The keys for which you are looking are on the shelf.

Die **Präposition** steht fast immer am **Ende** des Relativsatzes, also:
The man to whom I spoke is Mr Potter. ➧ *The man I spoke to is Mr Potter.*

15. Join the two sentences.

a) Simon lives in New York. He is Emma's penfriend.

b) Jennifer will be 16 next week. Her sister is in my class.

c) Darren joined our club. You met him yesterday.

____

d) These bikes are new. They belong to my friends.

____

Diese Relativsätze enthalten zusätzliche Informationen, die nicht unbedingt notwendig sind. Man nennt sie „nicht bestimmende Relativsätze" ***(non-defining relative clauses)***. Sie werden immer durch **Kommas** vom Hauptsatz getrennt. Man darf das Relativpronomen nicht weglassen und man darf nicht *that* anstelle von *who* bzw. *which* verwenden.

Vermischte Übungen

16. Fill in the correct pronouns if necessary.

a) After a month in England, Sabine joined ______________ a group of young people.

b) At the first meeting she introduced ______________ to all the boys and girls.

c) The group meets ______________ every Friday night.

d) They enjoy ______________ playing games and dancing.

e) Sabine wondered ______________ how she could have stayed a month with her first family.

f) She couldn't remember ______________ having met such nice people before.

g) They had a barbecue and Sabine and two other girls did all the preparations ______________.

h) When one of the girls was cutting the meat, she hurt ______________ with a sharp knife.

i) When the guests came, they helped ________________ to the food and drinks.

17. Say it in English.

a) Die Gäste fühlten sich sehr hungrig.

____

b) Herr Brown mischte sich selbst einen Cocktail.

____

c) Er konnte sich nicht erinnern, so viele nette Leute getroffen zu haben.

____

d) Sein Freund und er haben sich viele Jahre nicht gesehen.

____

e) Als es läutete, ging Herr Brown selbst zur Tür und öffnete.

____

18. Complete the sentences.

a) Simon, ____________ (?) father is an electrician, is my neighbour.

b) An electrician is a man ____________ (?) installs electric cables.

c) He often repairs TV sets and cassette recorders ____________ (?) don't work.

d) A hammer is a tool with ____________ (?) you can drive nails into wood.

e) The children saw some birds ____________ (?) feathers were blue and red.

19. Combine the following sentences.

a) The boy must stay in hospital. He broke his arm yesterday.

____

b) The young man wanted to speak to my sister. He rang up last night.

____

c) A car hit a cat. It was running across the road.

____

d) There were five men in the pub. They were dirty and dangerous.

____

e) They were waiting with Jake. His friend was a beggar.

____

f) The men saw two police cars. They stopped outside.

____

g) The police interviewed a man. They thought they had stolen a car.

____

20. Translate into English.

a) Das Buch, das ich gelesen habe, ist sehr spannend.

____

b) Die Geschichte, die Simon erzählt hat, ist nicht wahr.

____

c) Das Mädchen, mit dem Simon tanzte, kommt aus Frankreich.

____

d) Emma, deren Schwester gerade in Schottland ist, ist meine Freundin.

____

e) Der junge Mann, der bei dem Unfall verletzt wurde, ist im Krankenhaus.

____

21. Define the following words. Use relative clauses.

a) A manager ______________________________

b) Immigrants ______________________________

c) A housewife ______________________________

d) A dinosaur ______________________________

e) A burglar ______________________________

f) A skyscraper ______________________________

g) A pioneer ______________________________

h) A computer freak ______________________________

Prüfungsaufgaben

22. Complete the following text. Use the correct form of the words in brackets and find words of your own to replace the question marks.

a) Those ______________ (?) are skilled in older programming languages ______________ (?) are more likely to create problems in the new millennium have an advantage. (2)

b) Steven Spielberg made his own silent film "Amblin", in ______________ (?) two hitchhikers were trying to get to California. (1)

c) The boy runs a group ______________ (?) is called "Free the Children". (1)

d) He filled out his ticket order ______________ (?) amounted to $1,200. (1)

23. Language: Join the two sentences with a suitable relative clause.

a) The athletes arrived in their home town. They had competed in the Games. (2)

b) Rachel was dancing around happily. Her team had won a medal. (2)

c) The winner was interviewed after the competition. The competition had been really exciting. (2)

24. Define the following words in complete sentences.

a) A guard (3)

b) A debt (3)

c) An expert (3)

d) Confetti (3)

e) A teenager (3)

f) Commercials (3)

25. Translate into German.

a) The factory employs 13.000 people, who wear cheap plastic shoes, because none of them can afford the shoes they make. (4)

b) "To you in Europe the shoes we make have an image of freedom," she says. (3)

c) Fans will feel the enthusiasm that has made this sport the fastest-growing. (3)

____

d) Anna, whom teachers describe as extremely bright, is perhaps an exception. (3)

____

____

e) Her former English teacher says that there are children who have to stay on much longer. (3)

____

____

26. Underline the four mistakes and correct them. (4)

a) Mr Smith's car, who is standing outside, can do 120 miles an hour.

____

b) That's the bus for it I've been waiting for three hours.

____

c) Mr Parson, who is our English teacher, is a nice person.

____

d) Mr Parson, who I was speaking, has always got time for us.

____

e) The church you are looking at is a wonderful building.

____

f) Susy Brown we met at the party who is my girlfriend.

____

C Adjektiv – Adverb

Steigerung des Adjektivs

1. Fill in the adjectives in their correct forms or find other suitable words.

Four girls of the Abingdon Youth Club are preparing for a swimming competition.

a) Debby Pope is ____________ (tall) of the girls and she is an ____________ (excellent) swimmer. Debby is ____________ (old) than most other girls.

b) Rebecca Jackson is only ten years old and she is ____________ (young) of them. Of course, it is ____________ (difficult) for her to win than for the other girls because they are ____________ (strong) than her.

c) Lucy Parker is ____________ (pretty) girl, and she is wearing a ____________ (expensive) bathing costume than the others. Lucy has won ____________ (many) races this month than Rebecca, but at the moment she is not ______ good ______ last year.

d) Angela Miller is ____________ (ambitious) than her friends. Unfortunately, she had hurt herself last winter, and so she had ____________ (little) training than before and she took part in ____________ (few) competitions than she had expected.

e) For Patricia Baker ____________ (important) thing is to meet nice people. Her trainer says: "You could be much ____________ (good) if you tried harder."

Steigerung mit ***-er / -est*** *(big – bigger – the biggest)*, mit ***more / most*** *(difficult – more difficult – the most difficult)* oder unregelmäßig *(good – better – the best)*. Vergleich mit *(not)* ***as … as*** – (nicht) so … wie; mit ***than*** – als, z. B. *bigger than / more interesting than* – größer / interessanter als; höchste Steigerungsstufe: *the biggest / the most difficult* – der / die / das größte / schwierigste bzw. am größten / schwierigsten.

Bildung und Anwendung des Adverbs

2. Form the adverb.

a) Kate smiled ________________ (happy) when she saw Peter.

b) Jason sat in his room ________________ (quiet).

c) The girls spoke ______________________ (friendly).

d) Sarah can speak French ________________ (fluent).

e) Mark understands German ________________ (good).

f) Julie listened ________________ (careful) to her teacher.

g) Margaret came down from the tree ________________ (safe).

h) Paul could answer all questions ________________ (quick).

Du bildest das **Adverb** normalerweise so: **Adjektiv + *-ly* = Adverb**. Es gibt auch **Sonderformen**, wie *good – well, lovely – in a lovely way, fast – fast*. Beachte die Rechtschreibung, z. B. bei *safe – safely, easy – easily, automatic – automatically*!

3. Adjective and adverb. Fill in the correct form of the words.

a) easy English grammar is not always ______________. But you can ______________ do this exercise. It's an ______________ one.

b) angry Our teacher was ______________ today. He was shouting ______________ because we were so loud.

c) good Patricia can speak French ______________. Her Spanish is ______________, too.

d) usual What's your ______________ breakfast? – We ______________ have cornflakes with milk and toast with jam.

e) slow The bus was ______________. It went ______________ up the hill.

4. Translate into English.

Peter has come back from a language school in England.
Er berichtet:

a) Ich kann Englisch jetzt gut verstehen.
b) Meine Grammatik ist noch nicht perfekt.
c) Aber ich kann fließend sprechen.
d) Ich muss noch lernen, schwierige Wörter richtig zu schreiben.

a) ____

b) ____

c) ____

d) ____
____

5. Answer the questions.

a) How was school? – It was ______________________ (real, boring).

b) How were your teachers? – They were ______________________ (terrible, strict).

c) How was your English test? – It was ______________________ (extreme, difficult).

d) How did you come home? – Oh, that't a good question. Paul's father drove us home. He is an ________________ (awful, good) driver and he drove ________________ (real, quick).

Das **Adjektiv** bestimmt ein Substantiv oder Pronomen näher, z. B. *Peter is good, he is good*. Das **Adverb** beschreibt ein Verb, z. B. *Peter understands well*, ein Adjektiv, z. B. *(He is) really good* oder ein anderes Adverb, z. B. *(He drives) really quickly*. Beachte die **Schreibung**: *true – truly, extreme – extremely, terrible – terribly*!

6. Choose the right word. Fill in: **fair – fairly, hard – hardly, high – highly, near – nearly, late – lately.**

a) Simon jumped very ________________ in the athletics competition, and his result was ________________ appreciated.

b) Jonathan lives ________________ the bus stop, but he ________________ missed his bus this morning.

c) Jenny had to work ________________ for her exam and she could ________________ believe that she would pass it.

d) Claire got up ________________ this morning and was ________________ for school. This has happened several times ________________.

e) Andy saw a ________________ match. All the players were ________________ good and nobody was hurt.

Achte auf die verschiedene Bedeutung der sich ähnlich sehenden Adverbien, z. B. *hard* – hart, schwer; *hardly* – kaum.

Steigerung des Adverbs

7. Fill in the comparative forms.

a) Jane works carefully, but her sister works even ________________ than she does.

b) Bill runs very fast. He can run ______________ than his friends.

c) Jessica plays squash well. She can play it __________ than her little sister.

d) Jane's little brother eats very quickly. He eats ______________________ than the rest of the family.

e) Bill worked hard. In fact he worked _____________ than the other boys.

f) We arrived early. We arrived even ____________ than we had expected.

g) Tim takes sport seriously. He takes it ____________________ than other boys in his class.

8. **Form the superlative.**

a) Paul ran fast. He ran _____ ______________ of all competitors.

b) Susan likes swimming very much. She likes it _____ ___________ of all.

c) Jack went very far. He went _____ ______________ of all climbers.

d) Jenny sings beautifully. She sings _____ ____________________ of all.

e) Harry answered sensibly. He answered _____ ________________ of all.

f) Keith plays tennis well. He plays _____ ______________ of all his team.

Adverbien auf *-ly* werden mit ***more*** bzw. ***most*** gesteigert, z. B. *quickly – more quickly – most quickly*. Beachte **Sonderformen**, wie *well – better – best, badly – worse – worst*!

Adjektiv nach Zustandsverben

9. **Complete.**

a) Susan looks very ________________ (happy) today.

b) Her friend Sharon doesn't feel ______________ (sad) either.

c) The flowers in the vase smell ________________ (wonderful).

d) The birthday cake tastes ________________ (delicious).

e) The music sounds ______________ (good), but it is a bit ______________ (loud).

f) The little children were playing ______________ (happy) in the swimming pool.

g) When the lights went out they all felt their way ________________ (careful) in the dark.

h) Janet looks ______________ (nice) in her new dress.

Nach manchen Verben folgt das **Adjektiv** (nicht das Adverb!) – wenn sie einen **Zustand** oder eine **Eigenschaft** beschreiben. Unterscheide: *She looks happy.* – Sie sieht glücklich aus (= Sie ist glücklich). *She looks happily at him.* – Sie schaut ihn glücklich an.

Vermischte Übungen

10. Guided Writing.

Peter has invited his Scottish friend Ian to visit him next summer. Here he gives information on his home town. What does he write?

Peter berichtet ihm, dass …

a) München größer als Edinburgh ist;
b) es die größte Stadt in Bayern ist;
c) dort eines der bedeutendsten Museen Deutschlands ist;
d) vielleicht ein völlig neues Fußballstadion gebaut wird.

a) *Munich is* ________________________________

b) ________________________________

c) ________________________________

d) ________________________________

11. Translate into German.

Steven visited an Indian reservation in the U.S.A. and wrote some information to his penpal Hans.

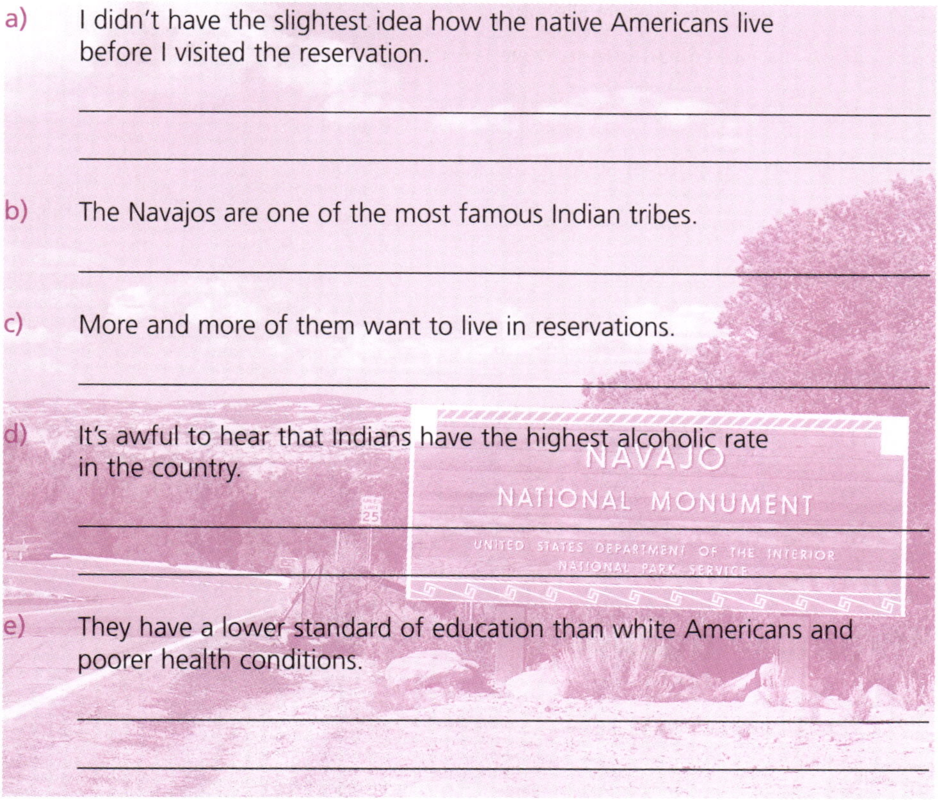

a) I didn't have the slightest idea how the native Americans live before I visited the reservation.

b) The Navajos are one of the most famous Indian tribes.

c) More and more of them want to live in reservations.

d) It's awful to hear that Indians have the highest alcoholic rate in the country.

e) They have a lower standard of education than white Americans and poorer health conditions.

12. Adjective or adverb? Write down the correct forms.

a) The Taylors like eating in pubs ________________ (regular).

b) They think a pub is a ________________ (popular) place where you can meet local people and enjoy the ________________ ________________ (extreme, warm) atmosphere there.

c) In their favourite pub "The Globe Inn" the food looks _________ (good) and it ________________ (real) tastes ________________ (excellent).

13. **Complete the text. Fill in adjectives or adverbs.**

Alan and Sheila are good friends.

a) Alan is good at most sports; he is even ________________ (good) than his elder brother and he often runs ________________ (quick) of all his class.

b) The two are good at school, because they work ________________ (quick) and ________________ (accurate) than other pupils.

c) Sheila's brother is the ____________ (bad) and ____________ (lazy) boy in the school, but she knows that he is ________________ (clever) than he shows.

d) David spends ________________ (much) of his time at the tennis court where he is one of the ____________ (good) players around. He is able to play very ____________ (hard) and ________________ (effective).

Prüfungsaufgaben

14. **Paraphrase the expressions in bold print.**

a) Twenty young people were **seriously injured** in an accident. (2)

They were ________________________________

b) Some boys, **especially** those who were standing had slight cuts. (1)

Some boys, ________________ *those who were standing,*

had slight cuts.

c) The ambulance arrived **at once.** (1)

It arrived ________________________________

15. Use words of the same families as the ones in brackets.

a) The captain of the Titanic was ____________________ (confidence) enough to believe that his ship was unsinkable. (1)

b) The __________________ (tragedy) accident happened 88 years ago. (1)

c) It was caused by a combination of poor planning and ________________ (fool) decisions. (1)

d) The ship was designed to be the ____________________ (safety) with its 16 watertight compartments. (1)

e) The passengers did not know how ____________________ (danger) icebergs are. (1)

16. Adjective or adverb? Write down the correct forms.

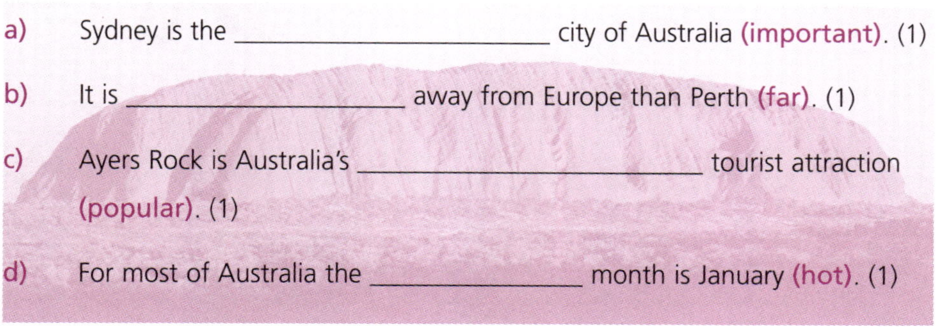

a) Sydney is the _______________________ city of Australia (important). (1)

b) It is ____________________ away from Europe than Perth (far). (1)

c) Ayers Rock is Australia's _________________________ tourist attraction (popular). (1)

d) For most of Australia the _______________ month is January (hot). (1)

17. Complete the following text. Use the correct form of the words in brackets and find a word of your own to replace the question mark.

The song "Tie a Yellow Ribbon ..." became a national symbol for Americans during the period form November 1979 to January 1981. They were waiting for 52 men and women to come home after they had been held prisoner in Iran for more a) ___________ (?) (1) a year. This was one of the b) ____________ (bad) periods in the US-Iranian relationship. But the positive aspect was that a c) ___________________ (real, remarkable) (2) spirit of d) ________________ (nation) (1) unity developed. People sent lots of letters to local newspapers and e) ____________ (many) (1) Americans than ever used a yellow ribbon to show their f) ____________ (deep) (1) love and care for people in need.

18. Writing a letter.

In a letter to his English pen-friend Sebastian tried to describe a dinosaur. Look at the picture and the German prompts and continue his letter.

Dear Chris,
Last week I watched "Jurassic Park" and I liked it very much. In a book I found some interesting information about these strange creatures. My favourite one was the brontosaurus.

- ▶ (ein riesiges Tier)
- ▶ (mindestens sechs Meter hoch und dreißig Meter lang)
- ▶ (dicke Beine wie ein Elefant)
- ▶ (und winziger Kopf)

The brontosaurus was a .____________________________________ (1)

It was ____ (3)

It had ____ (2)

and a ____________________________. (1)

19. Translate into German.

a) When Spielberg first thougt of making his most important film "Schindler's List", he was not sure if he could do it. (3)

____

____

b) Believing that other colleagues were better qualified for such a serious subject, he tried to sell the rights to more experienced directors. (4)

____

____

c) However, none of them was really interested. (2)

d) Many of his friends told him he would definitely fail. (2)

e) But the more doubts they expressed, the more certain Spielberg became. (2)

20. Underline the four mistakes and correct them. (4)

a) Susan thinks she is beautifuller than her friends.

b) She can cook very good.

c) Her pizza tastes well.

d) She can work very quickly.

e) She is quicker as most other girls.

f) Her friend David is the nicest boy around.

D Zeitformen

Simple present

1. **What they do at the weekend.**

a) Simon _______________ (play) football every afternoon.

b) Darren often _______________ (go) for long walks in the park.

c) Patrick _______________ (sit) most of the weekend in front of the TV.

d) Sheila and John _______________ (not watch) TV at all.

e) They sometimes _______________ (visit) their grandma on Saturday.

f) They ___________________ (not stay) there the whole afternoon.

2. **Say it in English.**

You talk to an American friend about your daily routine.

a) Ich stehe gewöhnlich um 7 Uhr auf.

____

b) Mein Schulbus geht um 20 vor 8.

____

c) Die erste Stunde beginnt immer um 8 Uhr.

____

d) Am Nachmittag gehe ich zum Fußballtraining.

____

e) Nach dem Abendessen sitze ich etwas vor dem Fernseher.

____

f) Am Samstag stehe ich nicht so früh auf, weil wir nicht in die Schule gehen.

____

____

Mit dem ***simple present*** berichtest du über etwas, das regelmäßig, oft oder gewohnheitsmäßig geschieht. Achte auf die Endung: *he comes, she goes, he cries*!

Present progressive

3. What are they doing?

a) Where is John? – He ____________ (tidy) his room.
He can't go out yet because it ____________ (rain) very hard.

b) Look, Darren ____________ (lie) on the sofa.
He ____________ (read) a book.

c) Martin and his father ____________ (work) in the garage.
They ____________ (repair) the bikes.

d) What can you hear? – Rachel ____________ (play) the guitar. Ann and Sheila ____________ (listen) to her.

e) What ____________ (you do)?
– I ____________ (repeat) the tenses.

4. Say it in English.

Rebecca is just talking to her German friend Kathi. She wants to know what they are doing.

a) Ich backe gerade einen Kuchen.

____

b) Mutter feiert ihren Geburtstag.

____

c) Susan ist beim Einkaufen.

____

d) Sie kauft Kaffee und Blumen.

____

e) Nur Paul macht nichts. – Oh doch, er spielt Tischtennis.

____

Mit dem ***present progressive*** drückst du aus, was gerade geschieht.
Vorsicht bei der Schreibung: *come* ➧ *coming, cut* ➧ *cutting;*
tidy ➧ *tidying*!

Simple past

5. What happened yesterday?

a) Yesterday Rebecca ____________ (decide) to go to a disco.

b) She ________________ (not walk); she __________ (go) by bus.

c) There ________ (not be) many people at the disco; it ______ (be) early.

d) Rebecca _______ (meet) a girlfriend and they _______ (sit) down.

e) The disc jockey _______ (tell) some jokes but she _______ ________________ (not understand) everything; the music ________ (be) too loud.

f) When a boy from her class _________ (enter) the room, they _________ (dance) together. They ________ (stay) there until 11 o'clock.

6. **Say it in English.**

Peter is back from England. He is reporting about his stay in London.

a) Letzte Woche waren wir in London.

____

b) Wir besuchten den „Rock Circus" und den „Dungeon of London".

____

c) Wir trafen nette Leute und gingen dann in ein Pub.

____

d) Wir aßen einige Sandwiches, aber wir bekamen kein Bier.

____

e) Der Wirt wollte unsere Ausweise sehen.

____

f) Dann sagte er: „Ihr seid zu jung für Alkohol."

____

Mit dem ***simple past*** berichtest du über Vorgänge, die in der Vergangenheit stattfanden. Achte auf **Signalwörter** wie *yesterday, last week, last year* und andere.

Past progressive

7. **What were Simon's friends doing yesterday in the afternoon?**

a) Yesterday afternoon Paul ____________________ (play) tennis.

b) His two sisters ____________________ (swim) in the pool.

c) Jenny ____________________ (read) a detective story.

d) Lucy ____________________ (knit) a pullover for her little sister.

e) Angela ____________________ (repair) her bike.

f) Jane and George ____________________ (prepare) for a maths test.

8. **Fill in: simple past or past progressive.**

a) It ____________________ (rain) this morning when the girls ____________________ (go) to the bus stop.

b) Darren ____________________ (write) a letter yesterday when his mother ____________________ (come) into his room and ____________________ (ask) him to help her.

c) When the school bell ____________________ (ring), all the pupils ____________________ (pack) their schoolbags and ____________________ (run) to the door.

d) Lucy ____________________ (read) a comic under her desk when her teacher ____________________ (come) and ____________________ (look) at her.

e) Patrick ____________________ (mend) his bike this afternoon when the telephone ____________________ (ring).

Mit dem ***past progressive*** drückst du aus, was zu einer bestimmten Zeit in der Vergangenheit gerade passierte, z. B. *He was playing tennis.* – Er hat (gerade) Tennis gespielt. Du kannst auch über eine stattfindende Handlung berichten, z. B. *he was mending* – er hat gerade repariert, die durch eine andere, die im ***simple past*** steht, z. B. *the telephone rang* – das Telefon läutete, unterbrochen wurde.

Present perfect

9. **Complete the sentences using the present perfect.**

a) Where is Debbie? – I ____________________ (not see) her since last week.

b) Bill likes Susan. – He ____________________ (know) her for two months.

c) The bike is all right. – I ____________________ (repair) it.

d) Lucy's room is in a mess. – She ____________________ (not tidy) it yet.

e) The Hubers know England well. – They ______________ (be) there ten times.

f) Steven is hungry. – He ______________ (not eat) anything since 8 o'clock.

10. Translate into English.

a) Julie ist traurig; sie hat ihre Schlüssel verloren.

b) Wir müssen warten; der Zug ist noch nicht angekommen.

c) Ist Patrick da? – Er ist gerade nach Hause gekommen.

d) Ich habe mein Zimmer aufgeräumt; jetzt kann ich spielen gehen.

e) Ich habe mein Fahrrad schon seit vier Jahren; es fährt immer noch gut.

f) Jenny war noch nie in London. Wie schade!

Mit dem ***present perfect*** berichtest du über etwas, das sich auf die Gegenwart auswirkt; was bisher oft geschehen ist bzw. noch nicht abgeschlossen ist oder sich zu einer unbestimmten Zeit in der Vergangenheit abgespielt hat. **Signale** sind z. B. *since 1999* – seit 1999; *for two days (now)* – (jetzt) seit zwei Tagen; *often* – schon oft; *never* – noch nie; *not yet* – bisher noch nicht.

Present perfect progressive

11. Use the present perfect progressive to complete the sentences.

a) I must stop now. I ____________________ (work) for five hours.

b) Tom is angry. He ____________________ (wait) for Andrea for over an hour.

c) The weather is awful. It ____________________ (rain) all day.

d) This is my parents' house. They ____________________ (live) here since 1999.

e) Jack is exhausted. He ____________________ (paint) the house all morning.

f) I ____________________ (try) to phone Martin, but the line was engaged.

g) Jackie likes music; she ____________________ (play) the piano for ten years.

12. Say it in English.

a) Wie lange lernst du schon Englisch? – Ich lerne es schon seit 5 Jahren.

____

____

b) Dieses Buch ist nicht neu. Wie lange benutzt du es schon? – Wir benutzen es schon seit Anfang des Schuljahres.

____

____

c) Dein kleiner Bruder ist so schmutzig. – Er hat den ganzen Morgen Fußball gespielt.

____

____

d) Dein Vater ist sehr müde. – Er hat den ganzen Tag im Garten gearbeitet.

____

____

Mit dem ***present perfect progressive*** berichtest du über etwas, das in der Vergangenheit begonnen hat und noch andauert (*since 8 o'clock* – seit 8 Uhr, *for two hours now* – jetzt schon seit zwei Stunden) oder schon lange andauert (z. B. *all morning* – schon den ganzen Morgen). Im Deutschen nimmst du oft das Präsens mit „schon"!

Past perfect

13. Answer the questions. Use the simple past and past perfect in your answers.

a) When did you go to bed last night? – (watch the film on TV)

I ______________ to bed after I ___________________ the film on TV.

b) When did Sheila drive to the youth club? – (finish her homework)

Sheila ______________ to the youth club after she __________________ her homework.

c) Why did Jane buy a new dress? – (want to go to a party)

Jane ______________ a new dress because she _____________________ to go to a party. But unfortunately she fell ill.

d) When did Kenneth phone his friend? – (go into town)

Kenneth ______________ his friend after he ____________________ into town.

e) When did the pupils begin to chatter? – (teacher leave the classroom)

The pupils ______________ to chatter after the teacher ______________ the classroom.

f) Why did Emma not come in time? – (miss the bus)

Emma ____________________ in time last night because she

______________________ the bus.

Mit dem ***past perfect*** berichtest du über weit zurückliegende Vorgänge. Das weiter zurückliegende Geschehen steht im ***past perfect***, das näher liegende im ***simple past***. Beachte mögliche Signale: *after* – nachdem, *when* – als, *before* – ehe, *because* – weil. Das ***past perfect*** verwendest du auch im if-Satz Typ 3: *I would have told you the answer if I had known it.*

Will-future

14. Make sentences using the elements given and add the will-future.

a) I'm sure / we / enjoy / our winter holidays

____

b) I hope / there be / enough snow

____

c) It / not be / easy to find / cheap accommodation

____

d) We / have to book / the rooms / next week

____

e) I / be / fifteen / in January

____

f) I think / we / have / a wonderful party / in the snow

____

15. Say it in English.

Translate the weather forecast for an English guest.

a) Morgen früh wird es in den Bergen bewölkt sein,
b) aber am Nachmittag wird die Sonne scheinen.
c) Übermorgen wird es wärmer sein, aber etwas windig.

d) Das Wetter wird sich in den nächsten Tagen wenig ändern.
e) Es wird sicher nicht regnen.

a) ______________________________

b) ______________________________

c) ______________________________

d) ______________________________

e) ______________________________

Du nimmst ***will-future*** für zukünftige Geschehen, die du nicht beeinflussen kannst. Hinweise sind z. B. *I think* – ich denke, *I hope* – ich hoffe, *I'm sure* – ich bin sicher, *I expect* – ich erwarte. Halte auseinander: ***I won't*** = *I will not* – ich werde nicht – *I want* – ich will!

Going to-future

16. What are they (not) going to do next week?

a) Mr Miller / paint his house

____

b) His wife / buy new curtains

____

c) The children / attend a language course

____

d) They / not watch TV / next Saturday

____

e) They / have / a big party / on Saturday night

____

f) They / have / lots of food and drinks

____

17. Say it in English.

Sage was deine Freunde vorhaben.

a) Paul: Ich will Martin treffen; wir haben vor, ein paar CDs zu kaufen.
b) Helen: Ich habe vor, mit meiner Mutter einkaufen zu gehen.
Ich brauche einen Mantel.
c) Barbara: Meine Schwester und ich werden Karten für das Musical kaufen.
Wir wollen die Vorstellung am Samstag besuchen.

a) Paul wants to meet Martin. They ______________________________

____

b) Helen ____

____

c) Barbara ____

____

Mit dem ***going to-future*** drückst du eine feste Absicht, einen Plan oder ein Vorhaben aus.

Vermischte Übungen

18. Write down the correct forms of the verbs given in brackets.

a) Patrick Miller, sixteen years old, has a girlfriend. He and Jennifer ____________________ (meet) ten months ago at their local youth centre, and they ____________________ (go) out ever since.

b) Patrick ____________________ (have) plenty of jobs already.

c) But now he ____________________ (work) in a supermarket, filling the shelves and sweeping the floor.

d) He only ____________________ (spend) some of the money on dances and drinks.

e) The rest ____________________ (save).

f) It ______________________ (help) to pay for his college education after leaving High School.

19. Fill in the correct tense.

Debbie is interviewing Patrick, a new pupil at Macclesfield High School.

Debbie: When ___________ you __________________ (arrive) in Macclesfield?

Patrick: My family __________________ (come) here last Saturday. At first everything ___________ (be) so new and exciting for me.

Debbie: Where ___________ (be) you from?

Patrick: Well, we __________________ (live) in a small town in Kent for ten years, but my father __________________ (lose) his job six months ago and, fortunately, he __________________ (find) a new one in Manchester.

Debbie: How ___________ you ___________ (like) Macclesfield?

Patrick. Well, I __________________ (not see) much of the town yet. I __________________ (spend) most of the time unpacking boxes.

Debbie: ___________ you __________________ (like) our school?

Patrick. Yes, I ___________. The classmates ___________ (be) very nice and Simon Moore often ________________ (help) me with the homework. We ________________ (use) other textbooks in Kent.

Debbie: What sports ___________ you __________________ (practise)?

Patrick: Well, I ____________ (be) good at hockey. I __________________ (play) it for five years now. I think I __________________ (join) the local club soon.

Debbie: ____________ (have) a good time here. Thank you.

Patrick: __________________ (?).

20. Guided Writing.

a) David begrüßt Steven und fragt nach seinen Plänen für die Sommerferien.

____

____?

b) Steven sagt, dass er letztes Jahr in Kanada war und dass ihm die Reise sehr viel Spaß bereitet hat. Er möchte wieder nach Kanada.

____

____

____

c) David sagt, dass er bisher noch nicht in Kanada gewesen ist. Er hoffe aber, in zwei Jahren seine Tante in Toronto besuchen zu können.

____

____

____

Achte auf die **Signale**:
last year – letztes Jahr ▶ ***simple past***,
not … yet – (bisher) noch nicht ▶ ***present perfect***,
in two years – in zwei Jahren ▶ ***future***.

Prüfungsaufgaben

21. Fill in the correct forms of the verbs given in brackets. (4)

a) The city of Sydney __________________ **(hold)** the Olympic Games in 2000.

b) The Olympic Games of 1992 ______________________ **(take place)** in Barcelona.

c) Since 1896 a lot of athletes from all over the world ____________________ **(compete)** in Olympic Games.

d) Usually millions of people ___________________ **(watch)** the events on TV.

22. Complete the following text. Use the correct form of the words in brackets.

Sheila Wright **a)**___________________ **(live)** (1) in Cheltenham. She **b)** _______________________________ **(just, come)** (2) back from a school trip to London. She **c)** _______________________ **(wear)** (1) a new pair of shoes. Looking at them her mother says, "Why **d)** _____________________ **(you, buy)** (1) these shoes in London?" Sheila replies that they are "Doc Martens", and they **e)** _______________________ **(invent)** (1) in the forties by Claus Maertens who **f)** ____________________ **(experiment)** (1) with old tyres to make a pair of shoes after **g)** _________________________ **(injure)** (1) his foot. He **h)** __________________________ **(succeed, get)** (2) a patent on the heavy shoe with the thick sole. Since the eighties the "DMs" **i)** ___________________________ **(become)** (1) a fashion item.

23. The Iceberg Comes

When Edith Brown Hausman last saw her daddy 88 years ago he was standing on the deck of the Titanic, smoking a cigar and smiling at his wife and daughter. "I'll see you in New York", he said confidently, as his family was taken to Lifeboat No. 14. Edith and her mother watched as the band played a hymn, the lights went out and in a terrible roar everything on the supership seemed to break loose. And then it was gone, along with Mr Brown and over 1,522 other souls. …
Even today, the Titanic tragedy lives on in the human imagination and in books, films, plays and even on the Internet. One of the reasons is that it is a story of superlatives. …

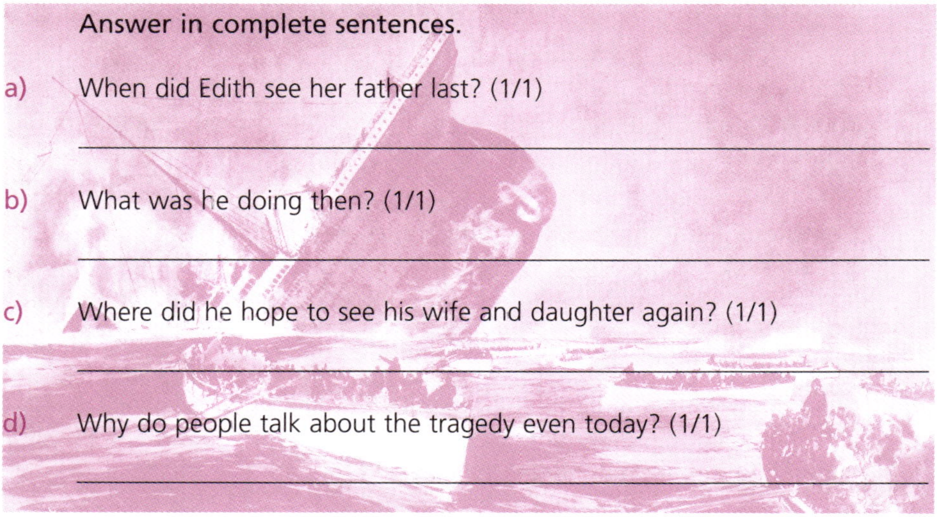

Answer in complete sentences.

a) When did Edith see her father last? (1/1)

____

b) What was he doing then? (1/1)

____

c) Where did he hope to see his wife and daughter again? (1/1)

____

d) Why do people talk about the tragedy even today? (1/1)

____

24. Personal question. Write complete sentences.

What are your personal hopes or fears for the future? You may use these words: **job, partner, family – enjoy, find, get on well with.** (2/2)

____

____

____

____

25. Guided Writing.

You want to invite your American friend Joey to come with you on the luxury liner "Hanseatic". You are now writing a fax to him talking about the notes you have made on the German brochure. (10)

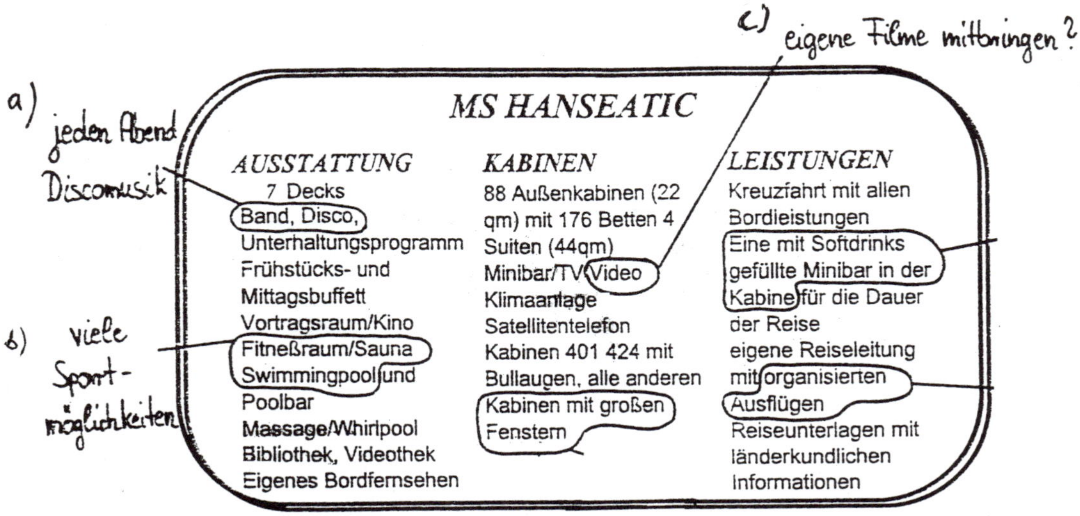

Dear Joey,

I a) ______________________ (write) you this letter because I b) ______________________ (win) a trip for two people on the "Hanseatic" and I c) ______________________ (like) to invite you to come with me. There d) ______________ (be) a disco every evening and there e) ______________ (be) lots of sports facilities. There f) ______________ (be) a video recorder in our room and we g) ______________________ (take) our own films with us. I hope you h) ______________________ (come) with me. I i) ______________________ (look forward) j) ________________ (see) you on the "Hanseatic".

Best wishes, Dominik.

26. Translate into German.

a) After four years of involuntary absence, Vingo S. was welcomed home spectacularly by his wife and three kids. (4)

____

____

b) It was a happy ending to a story that had taken a tragic turn four years before, when Vingo was imprisoned. (3)

c) What was the crime he had committed? (1)

d) He worked in his uncle's bank, and when his uncle suddenly disappeared, he was accused of being a criminal. (4)

27. **Underline the five mistakes and correct them.** (5)

a) Jennifer has visited Rome last summer.

b) Darren has been away since Monday.

c) Keith is a member of our youth club for two years now.

d) Helen is going to buy a new shirt tomorrow.

e) Angela gave the video back after she has seen it.

f) When Sheila entered the room, Patrick slept.

g) Barbara listens to the radio just now.

E Fragesätze

Entscheidungsfragen

1. Questions about school.

a) ______________________________?

– Yes, school begins at eight o'clock

b) ______________________________?

– Yes, there are lessons every afternoon.

c) ______________________________?

– Yes, we have lunch at school.

d) ______________________________?

– No, we don't go to school on Saturday.

e) ______________________________?

– No, I haven't visited our twin town in Germany yet.

2. Guided Writing: Asking questions.

Julia is a new pupil in your class. You want to know whether she …

a) is interested in sports
b) likes tennis
c) saw the match last night
d) wants to play a game against you
e) can meet you at ten o'clock tomorrow.

a) ______________________________

b) ______________________________

c) ______________________________

d) ______________________________

e) ______________________________

Entscheidungsfragen haben kein Fragewort. Die Antwort lautet ***yes*** oder ***no***. Du nimmst ein vorhandenes **Hilfsverb** (z. B. *be, can*) oder das Ersatzhilfsverb *do / does* bzw. *did.*

Fragen mit einem Fragewort

3. **Ask for the information which you can't see.**

a) The first lesson begins at ??? every morning.

______________________________?

b) The pupils can buy refreshments in the ???.

______________________________?

c) Andy went to the club last week because ???.

______________________________?

d) Most pupils work very ???.

______________________________?

e) Homework takes ??? hours a day.

______________________________?

f) The school uniform costs ??? £.

______________________________?

g) Jennifer came to school by ???.

______________________________?

h) Darren must get up at ??? every morning.

______________________________?

Diese Fragen beginnen mit einem **Fragewort**: *when* – wann?; *where* – wo?; *how* – wie?, *how much* – wie viel?; *how many* – wie viele?; *why* – warum? Nach dem Fragewort folgt ein Hilfsverb (z. B. *can*) oder das Ersatzhilfsverb *do / does / did.*

4. Ask for the object of the sentences.

a) Simon wrote a letter.

____?

b) Fred likes hockey.

____?

c) Jane bought a camera.

____?

d) Julia and Emma will visit their aunt.

____?

e) They have read a French newspaper.

____?

f) Oliver helps his mother in the afternoon.

____?

g) Darren lost his camera.

____?

Mit *who* (auch: *whom*) – wen? bzw. *what* – was? fragst du nach dem **Objekt** des Satzes. Nach dem Fragewort folgt ein Hilfsverb (z. B. *have, will, can*) oder das Ersatzhilfsverb *do / does / did*.

5. Ask for the information that you can't see.

a) ??? loves Julia.

____?

b) ??? went to Italy in her summer holidays.

____?

c) The ??? happened in front of the school.

____?

d) The ??? begins at nine o'clock.

____?

e) ???'s friend plays the guitar.

____?

f) Bus ??? goes to the railway station.

____?

g) ??? children came to the birthday party.

____?

Mit *who* – wer?; *which* – welcher?; *which of you* – wer von euch?; *what* – was?; *whose* – wessen? fragst du nach dem **Subjekt** des Satzes. Es gibt keine Umschreibung mit *do / does / did*!

Verneinte Fragen

6. **Make up negative questions.**

a) Who plays cricket?

____?

b) Which of you knows the answer?

____?

c) Why did Jack stay in Dublin?

____?

d) When can Sheila go home?

____?

e) Which books belong to you?

____?

f) How many of you like rugby?

____?

g) Who came to the barbecue?

____?

Bei **verneinten Fragen – auch bei verneinten Subjektfragen** – gilt das Gleiche wie bei verneinten Aussagen: Du brauchst in jedem Fall ein Hilfsverb (z. B. *can*) oder ein Ersatzhilfsverb *do / does / did*. Also: *Who comes?* ➧ *Who doesn't come? What happened?* ➧ *What didn't happen?*

Fragen mit nachgestellter Präposition

7. Ask for the words in bold print.

a) Geoff comes from **Manchester**.

____?

b) He is good at **music and sport**.

____?

c) He goes to **a large comprehensive** school.

____?

d) The old Rover belongs to **his father**.

____?

e) He bought it from **an old lady**.

____?

f) He sometimes listens to **classical music**.

____?

g) Geoff and his friends are talking about **their summer holidays**.

____?

h) They are afraid of **too much rain**.

____?

Du beginnst mit dem Fragewort und stellst **die Präposition ans Ende**. Beachte den Unterschied zum Deutschen:

Who is it ***from?***
Von wem ist es?

What are you talking ***about?***
Über was redet ihr?

Angehängte Kurzfragen *(question tags)*

8. Add a question tag.

a) Julia is sixteen now, ______________________________?

b) She has got three brothers, ______________________________?

c) She can speak German, ______________________________?

d) Jason isn't very tall, ______________________________?

e) They cycle to school, ______________________________?

f) Julia doesn't play the violin, ______________________________?

g) Martin went to London last week, ______________________________?

h) He'll come to Germany next summer, ______________________________?

Auf eine **positive Aussage** folgt eine **negative Kurzfrage** (z. B. *She is* ➧ *isn't she?*). Auf eine **negative Aussage** folgt eine **positive Kurzfrage** (z. B. *He isn't* ➧ *is he?*). Du nimmst ein Hilfsverb bzw. *do / does / did* anstelle eines Vollverbs.

Vermischte Übungen

9. An interview with a boy from Scotland.

Ian is staying in your town for a while. Ask him some questions using the elements given:

a) What time / get up / every morning?

____

b) How / get to school?

______

c) Like / school?

______

d) What / do / in your spare time?

______

e) Which / favourite soccer team?

______

f) know / a German football club?

______

g) Where / learn / German?

______

h) Which places / see / so far?

______

10. An American girl is visiting your class. Ask her some questions.

Du möchtest gern wissen, …

a) wo sie herkommt;

______

b) ob sie Geschwister hat;

______

c) wie ihr Deutschland gefällt;

______

d) was ihr an einer deutschen Schule nicht gefällt;

______

e) ob sie schon früher in Europa war;

______

f) was ihre Hobbys sind;

____

g) wie lange sie bleiben wird;

____

h) ob sie einen Freund hat.

____

11. An interview for a job.

Mrs Collins is asking Katie a few personal questions. What does she say?

Mrs Collins wants to know …

a) whether Katie knows any foreign languages;

____

b) what schools she went to;

____

c) which her favourite subjects at school were;

____

d) which subjects she didn't like at all;

____

e) where she usually spends her weekends;

____

f) why she would like to become a secretary;

____

g) how she is going to come to the office every day;

____

h) when she will be able to start work.

____

12. **You have decided to visit London.Your pen-friend advised you to buy a special Travelcard because it is the most economical way to travel in London. But you need some more information.**

You would like to know …

a) the price for the ticket;

____?

b) where to buy it;

____?

c) when to use it;

____?

d) whether your friend has ever used the Travelcard herself.

____?

Prüfungsaufgaben

13. **A famous athlete opens a new Fitness Centre in his home town. You get the chance to talk to him. Write down your questions.** (4)

You want to know …

a) when he won his first medal;

____

b) whether he knows any sportsmen who take drugs;

____

c) why he decided to become an athlete;

____

d) how long he practises every day.

____

14. You are driving along Route 66. You talk to the attendant at a gas station and you ask him about … (4)

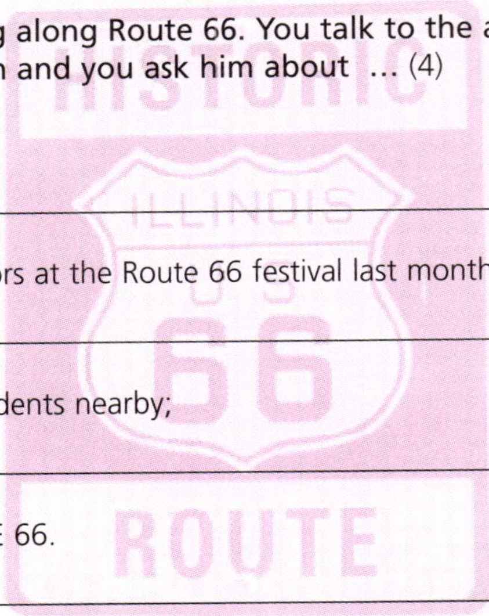

a) motels;

____

b) number of visitors at the Route 66 festival last month;

____

c) any serious accidents nearby;

____

d) TV series ROUTE 66.

____

15. Guided Writing.

Michael, a German computer freak, is walking around a computer fair in Munich. He is talking to Mr Best, the representative of an American firm.

a) Mr Best (fragt, ob er ihm behilflich sein könnte): (2)

______________________________?

b) Michael (erkundigt sich nach Sonderangeboten): (2)

______________________________?

c) Michael (will wissen, wie viel das neue Fremdsprachenprogramm kostet): (2)

______________________________?

d) Michael (möchte herausfinden, ob Mr Best es empfehlen könne): (2)

______________________________?

e) Michael (fragt, welche Übungen Kunden in den USA bevorzugen): (2)

______________________________?

16. Defective dialogue.
Ask the questions.

The Oxford College Magazine interviewed students on their job activities. Write down the questions. The answers are here: (6)

a) ____?

Because I don't get enough money from my parents to buy clothes I like.

b) ____?

Of course, there are. In my store we always call the police. Shoplifters are a nuisance.

c) ____?

My job – it's mostly exciting and well-paid.

17. Underline the mistakes and correct them. (5)

Ask your colleague:

a) Who do you live?

____

b) How many brothers and sisters do you have?

____

c) What do you at the weekend?

____

d) Can you speak French?

____

e) Which sport like you?

____

F Modalverben

Fähigkeit: *can – could – be able to*

1. Fill in: **can – can't – couldn't – be able to**.
Foreign languages

a) Catherine has a penfriend in Hamburg. She ______________ speak a little German, but she ______________ speak French.

b) She wants to go to a language school and hopes that she ________________________ speak French, too.

c) When her brother was ten, he ______________ speak German; he started to learn it when he was twelve.

d) Their parents ______________ only speak English because they have never learnt another language. So they ______________ speak German or French.

e) When they were in Paris last summer they ______________ understand what people were saying to each other.

2. Say it in English.

a) Ich kann dir leider nicht helfen.

____

b) Gestern konnte ich nicht Tennis spielen, weil es geregnet hat.

____

c) Ich habe Tom noch nicht anrufen können; ich kann seine Telefonnummer nicht finden.

____

d) Nächsten Samstag werde ich nicht zum Training kommen können.

____

e) Ich könnte dir helfen, wenn du mich vorher anrufst.

____

Für **„können"** kannst du im ***present*** *can* oder *am / is / are able to* nehmen. **Die anderen Zeiten** bildest du mit der entsprechenden Form von *be able to*. ***Could*** heißt meist „könnte"; *could not* bedeutet – je nach Zusammenhang – „konnte nicht" oder „könnte nicht".

Erlaubnis – Verbot: *can – can't – mustn't*

3. Fill in: **can – may – can't – mustn't – be allowed to.**

a) ____________ we play in the garden? – Yes, of course.
But you ____________ be too loud; grandmother wants to have a rest.

b) Don't drive so fast! You ____________ drive faster than twenty miles an hour near the the school.

c) You ________ sit here, but you ______________ smoke in this room.

d) Excuse me, ____________ I take the magazine? – Oh yes, you ____________ keep it.

e) Yesterday there was a big birthday party. The children ______________ stay up late.

f) Next summer Helen ________________________ go on holiday without her parents.

g) We came to the beach two days ago, but we ____________________ ____________ (go) swimming yet because the sea is very rough.

4. Translate.

Susan schreibt ihrer Brieffreundin in Schottland:

a) Während der Woche darf ich abends nicht ausgehen.

____

b) Am Wochenende darf ich bis 10 Uhr wegbleiben.

____

c) Letzten Freitag durfte ich ins Konzert gehen.

____

d) Nächstes Jahr werde ich mit meinen Freundinnen nach Italien fahren dürfen.

____

Für **„dürfen"** kannst du im ***present*** *can* oder *am / is / are allowed to* nehmen. Für die anderen Zeiten brauchst du die entsprechende Form von *be allowed to*. Ein **Verbot** drückst du mit *can't* aus, ein ausdrückliches Verbot mit *mustn't* – nicht dürfen. Mit *may* – dürfen, fragst du sehr höflich, ob du darfst.

Notwendigkeit, Zwang: *must – need not – have to*

5. Complete.

a) Today is Friday. Mrs Fleming has been ill since Monday. Her husband and the children __________________ do a lot of work in the house.

b) Yesterday Darren __________________ cook dinner.
– ______ he __________________ do the washing too? –
No, he __________.

c) On Wednesday Pamela __________________ water the flowers in the garden, but she __________________ cut the lawn.

d) Mr Fleming __________________ go shopping all the week.

e) Mrs Fleming __________________ go to her doctor next Monday to have a check up and get some medicine if necessary.

6. **Say it in English.**

a) Wir müssen diesen Monat viel lernen.

____

b) Gestern mussten wir einen langen Aufsatz schreiben.

____

c) Morgen werden wir eine schwierige Matheaufgabe machen müssen.

____

d) Wir haben seit zwei Wochen ein Projekt vorbereiten müssen.

____

e) Am Freitag müssen wir nicht zur Schule kommen.

____

Für „müssen" kannst du im ***present*** *must* oder *has to / have to* nehmen;
„nicht müssen" heißt *need not* oder *doesn't have to / don't have to.*
Für die anderen Zeiten nimmst du die entsprechende Form von *have to.*

Möglichkeit, Wahrscheinlichkeit: *may – might*

7. **Use may – might – may have – might have.**

a) Bill isn't at home. He ________________ be in the fitness centre.
He's quite often there.

b) Jane isn't on the bus. She ________________________ gone by bike.
It isn't raining.

c) Kate ________________ lend you her racket, but I don't think she will.

d) Tom ________________________ helped you if you had asked him.

e) You ________________ be right, but I don't think they will believe you.

f) Darren's team lost the match. They ________________________ won if
they hadn't been so ineffective.

May bedeutet „kann“ bzw. „vielleicht“, z. B. *it may rain soon* – vielleicht regnet es bald; es kann bald regnen. Mit ***might*** – könnte vielleicht, drückst du eine recht unsichere Vermutung aus. Beachte die Frage: *May I sit here?* – Darf ich hier sitzen?

Ratschlag, Verpflichtung: *should – ought to*

8. Use **should – shouldn't – should have – shouldn't have**.

a) The music is very loud. You ______________________ turn the loudspeaker down.

b) Cigarettes are not good for your health. You ______________________ smoke so much.

c) Your room is in a mess. You ___________________________ tidy it.

d) You're late. You ___________________________ taken an earlier bus.

e) Your keys are gone. You ___________________________ left them on the fence.

f) Your essay isn't good. You ___________________________ tried harder.

Should heißt „sollte“. Für *should* kannst du *ought to* nehmen. Mit *should + past participle* bzw. *ought to + past participle* drückst du aus, dass etwas hätte sein sollen.

Vermischte Übungen

9. Fill in: **can – mustn't – needn't**.

a) You ______________ stay at home, Darren. You ______________ come with me. I ______________ do the shopping by myself.

b) We're early. We ____________ run so fast; we _____________ walk slowly.

c) It isn't cold outside. So we ______________ put on our coats. We ______________ wear our jackets.

d) It's a very important meeting. You ______________ forget to come.

e) ______________ we park here? Yes, of course, but you ______________ forget to be back before eight o'clock when we close the gate.

f) Jennifer ______________ be back home by 10 o'clock. She ______________ be late because her dad will be angry.

10. Can you give advice?

a) Peter can't swim. ➧ He __________________ jump into deep water.

b) Paul has missed his school bus. ➧ He __________________ got up earlier.

c) There are no lessons on Saturday. ➧ You __________________ get up early.

d) Sussex Road is very busy. ➧ Pedestrians __________________ cross it; they __________________ use the subway.

e) When you go to an interview for a job you __________________ wear a T-shirt and jeans. ➧ You ________________ put on a jacket and trousers.

f) You see this traffic sign:

➧ You __________________ drive very carefully, and you __________________ drive too fast.

11. Translate into German.

a) May we sit here? – Oh, yes.

____

b) It may rain tomorrow. Shall we change our plans?

____

c) Could you show me the bus stop, please?

d) Jennifer could not come to our party because she was ill last week.

e) You mustn't leave the door open, Barbara. It's windy.

f) You needn't help me, Darren. I can do it myself.

12. Translate into German: modal verb + have been.

a) I can't find my key. I must have forgotten it.

b) It's a pity you dropped the vase. You should have been more careful.

c) You needn't have come so early. The meeting starts in half an hour.

d) I waved at Peter in the street but he didn't react; he may have been in a hurry.

e) The accident was awful. It might have been even worse if the ambulance hadn't come quickly.

f) Sheila can't have forgotten the date, she is so reliable.

Du willst sagen, dass etwas hätte sein sollen – *should have been / ought to have;* …, sein müssen – *must have* …; vielleicht sein sollen – *may have … / might have* … bzw. sein können – *can have … (been).*

Prüfungsaufgaben

13. Personal questions.

a) What can you do to protect the environment? Name two different aspects and explain. (lights? electricity?) (2/2)

b) Give a brief description of what life might be like in the year 3000? (transport? health?) (2/2)

c) What do you have to do when there is a fire alarm at your school? (2/2)

14. It is important for every Californian to know how to reduce dangers. Look at the signs and write down what you must do or should avoid before, during and after an earthquake, and say why.

Before:

a) 

You ____________ have a First Aid Kit so that you ____________ help injured people. (3)

During:

b) 

You ____________ smoke or light a match because the flames ____________ cause an explosion. (3)

After:

c) 

You ____________ listen to the news to get information about what to do next. (3)

15. Translate into German.

This is a letter which an American housewife wrote to her mother to complain about her husband:

a) Dear Mum, you may remember that Jack decided to buy a computer three months ago. (3)

____

____

b) Since then there has been a radical change in his attitude to his family. (2)

____

____

c) Every day he spends hours and hours on his computer trying out new programs. (2)

____

____

d) Even on the weekends Jack cannot resist sitting in front of the monitor. (2)

____

____

e) I think it might be a good idea to ask Uncle Herbert for advice. (2)

____

f) He should be able to tell me what to do. (2)

____

16. Underline four mistakes in the German translation and correct them. (5)

a) You mustn't take this bus. Du musst diesen Bus nicht nehmen.

b) It may snow tomorrow. Es darf morgen schneien.

c) Can we stay here? Dürfen wir hier bleiben?

d) Could you help me, please? Konntest du mir bitte helfen?

e) He should come earlier. Er soll früher kommen.

G Passiv

Simple present – present progressive

1. Say what happens or is happening.

a) The lawn ______________________ (cut) at the moment.

b) All the playing fields ______________________ (cut) every week.

c) Cars ______________________ (repair) at a garage.

d) I can't visit you because my car ______________________ (repair).

e) You mustn't enter the room. A candidate ______________________ (test).

f) The candidates ______________________ (not, test) at the same time.

Simple past – past progressive

2. Say what happened or was happening.

a) John couldn't go swimming last week because the swimming pool ______________________ (clean).

b) The room is not dirty. It ______________________ (clean) yesterday.

c) The bridge ______________________ (build) when we wanted to cross the river.

d) A lot of bridges ______________________ (build) in the past.

e) In the little cafe snacks ______________________ (serve) all the day.

f) When we came in some of the customers ______________________ (serve).

Du bildest das **Passiv** mit einer Form von ***to be*** und dem ***past participle*** (Partizip Perfekt / 3. Form des Verbs). Du kannst auch **modale Hilfsverben** und *be* und das *past participle* verwenden. Die ***progressive form*** (= Verlaufsform) bildest du im *present* mit *am / are / is + being + past participle* und im *past* mit *was / were + being + past participle.*

Present perfect

3. Say what has happened.

a) Ten thousand pounds ______________________ (steal) from the bank.

b) This letter ______________________ (write) perfectly.

c) I hope only correct answers ______________________ (give).

d) All their problems ______________________ (solve).

e) A lot of work ______________________ (do) today.

f) Smoking in schools ______________________ (not, allow) for some years.

g) My friend lost his bike. It ______________________ (not, find) yet.

h) Angela ______________________ (never, invite) to a party.

Will-future

4. Say what will happen.

a) My car ________________________ (not, repair) until next week.

b) The final match ________________________ (show) on TV.

c) Difficult questions ____________________ (ask) by the examiner.

d) A lot of windows ________________________ (smash) by the hooligans.

e) A new supermarket ________________________ (open) next month.

f) All my friends ________________________ (invite) to my party.

g) The building ________________________ (not, complete) until next year.

h) Angela's film ________________________ (develop) by Friday.

Modalverben

5. Say what can, must, should, ought to, has to be done.

a) Your car is dirty. It ________________________ (should wash).

b) The door ________________________ (cannot, shut). The lock is broken.

c) Sheila's room ________________________ (ought to, tidy). It's in a mess.

d) There were a lot of clouds. The mountains ______________________ ____________ (could not, see).

e) Grandma is ill. She ______________________ (must, look after).

f) Susan ______________________ (might, invite) to John's party.

g) The old house is a ruin. It ______________________ (have to, pull down) next year.

h) Chinese is a difficult language. It ______________________ (cannot, learn) easily.

i) Tony ______________________ (not, ought to, laugh at) by the other boys.

j) This kind of work ______________________ (can, only, do) with the help of computers.

k) The house ______________________ (must, sell) by the end of summer.

l) The washing-up ______________________ (have to, do) by the boys.

m) The private office ______________________ (must, not, enter).

n) The fire ______________________ (could, not, put out) because there wasn't enough water.

Vermischte Übungen

6. **Make sentences in the passive. Find the right tense.**

a) English ______________________ (understand) all over the world.

b) Angela ______________________ (invite) to our party next week.

c) A thriller ______________________ (show) on TV last night.

d) A lot of money ______________________ (earn) in professional football.

e) The match ______________________ (win) by our team next Sunday.

f) The Brown's house ______________________ (build) twenty years ago.

g) The new building ______________________ (not, finish) yet.

h) Our new school ______________________ (finish) by next summer.

i) This problem ______________________ (must, discuss) by our headmaster tomorrow.

j) German ______________________ (not, teach) in all English schools.

k) Bavarian beer ______________________ (always, be) famous.

l) Great progress ______________________ (make) in computer technology in recent years.

m) I can't tell you the time. My watch ______________________ (repair).

n) We couldn't cross the river because a new bridge ______________________ (build). The old one was dangerous.

Achte auf Signalwörter (z. B. *next Sunday, not yet, last night*) und bilde dann die richtige Zeitform.

7. Active or passive?

a) The first Olympic Games of modern times ____________________ (to take place) in Paris.

b) In ancient Greece the Games ____________________ (to celebrate) in the form of religious festivals.

c) The earliest Olympic Games ____________________ (to take place) about 776 BC.

d) There ______________ (to be) originally four towns where the Games ____________________ (to hold).

e) The events ____________________ (to include) all sorts of competitions, like running, throwing, wrestling.

f) The winners ____________________ (to treat) like modern professionals.

g) Baron de Coubertin ____________________ (to renew) the old tradition.

h) Since then the Olympic Games ____________________ (to hold) again every four years with only two exceptions during the two World Wars.

i) When a city ____________________ (to apply) for the Games, a lot of sports facilities ____________________ (must, to build).

j) Since 1896 more and more athletes ____________________ (to invite) to take part in the competitions.

k) Today all big sports events ____________________ (to show) on television.

Beachte Signalwörter (z. B. Zeitangaben oder *since*) und achte auf den Sinnzusammenhang, bevor du dich für die richtige Zeitform und für Aktiv oder Passiv entscheidest.

8. Translate into German.

a) Mrs Carter was offered a better job.

b) Last night the doctor was sent for.

c) The team will be offered a great chance.

d) Mr Johnson is supposed to fly to Paris next week.

e) It was said that Mr Brown would find another job.

Manche Passivsätze kannst du mit „man“ im Deutschen wiedergeben.

9. Say it in English.

a) Sage, dass man eine Fähre nach England sehr früh buchen muss.

b) Sage, dass man dir einen Brief schrieb.

c) Sage, dass man dir ein gutes Hotel angeboten hat.

d) Sage, dass man dir bald ein gutes Angebot schicken wird.

e) Sage, dass man deinen Freund ebenfalls eingeladen hat.

Beachte, dass gewöhnlich das **indirekte Objekt** (z. B. *I, my friend*) zum **Subjekt** im Passivsatz wird.

Prüfungsaufgaben

10. Put in the correct forms of the words in brackets or find a word of your own.

a) Even as a child Carl Sagan ____________________ (fascinate) by the night sky. (2)

b) When Sagan was 12 years old he ____________________ (???) by his grandfather what he wanted to be. (2)

c) Although many of the watertight compartments ____________________ (damage), most passengers had no idea … (2)

d) She ____________________ (interview) by a reporter from London. (2)

e) The following sentences ____________________ (take) from a novel. (2)

f) She really liked the voice that ____________________ (chose) for the computer. (2)

11. Translate into German.

a) You are more likely to be believed later. (3)

____

b) I have made a film that has been called the most expensive one. (4)

____

____

c) Most stunt people were seriously injured. (3)

____

d) Since then the Olympic Games have been held again. (3)

____

e) Eni is paid 25 cents an hour. (2)

____

f) They are often forced to work until midnight. (2)

g) Two fingers were cut off. (2)

12. Underline the five mistakes and correct them. (5)

a) Shorts and T-shirts is worn in summer.

b) The fish is being frying in a pan.

c) The new potatoes will be planted in spring.

d) Buses are drove by bus-drivers.

e) Cold drinks must keeping in a fridge.

f) Tony sagt, er sei ein guter Spieler. (= Tony is said to be a good player.)

H Gerund – Infinitiv

Gerund als Subjekt oder Objekt eines Satzes

1. Complete.

a) Do you like ____________________ (smoke), Terry?
– No, ____________________ (smoke) is dangerous for my health.

b) Do you enjoy ____________________ (read) comics, Steven?
– Yes, I do. ____________________ (read) comics is great fun.

c) Do you mind ____________________ (get) up early, Janet? – No. I don't mind ____________________ (get) up early, but not at the weekend.

d) Is ____________________ (play) tennis your hobby, Mike?
– Not really. I prefer ____________________ (cycle).

2. **Translate into English. Use a gerund in each sentence.**

a) Tennis spielen ist Rebeccas Lieblingssport.

____

b) Es macht ihr nichts aus im Regen zu spielen.

____

c) Simon liest gerne Abenteuergeschichten.

____

d) Aber sein Hobby ist das Gitarrespielen.

____

e) Peter kommt oft zu spät in die Schule. Er hasst es, früh aufzustehen.

____

____

Du wiederholst das **Gerund** als **Subjekt**, z. B. ***Smoking** is dangerous.* – Rauchen ist gefährlich. bzw. als **Objekt** eines Satzes nach bestimmten Verben, z. B. *He enjoys **smoking*** – Er hat Freude am Rauchen / Er hat Freude daran zu rauchen.

Gerund nach Präpositionen

3. Complete: verb + preposition + gerund.

a) Patrick apologised ________ __________________ (come) late.

b) Dawn dreams ________ __________________ (travel) to California.

c) Steven insisted ________ __________________ (pay) for the ice cream.

d) Matthew looks forward _______ _______________ (work) in his holidays.

e) James was fined ________ __________________ (drive) too fast.

f) Lindsey succeeded _______ __________________ (win) the tennis match.

g) Simon is thinking ________ __________________ (go) on a cycling tour.

h) Emma objects _______ _________________ (write) the essay once again.

Du verwendest hier das Gerund nach bestimmten **Verben + Präposition**, z. B. *apologise + for* + ing-Form. Lerne diese Wendungen immer mit der dazugehörigen Präposition.

4. Complete: adjective + preposition + gerund.

a) Simon was proud ________ ________________ (be) champion of his club.

b) Alan is afraid ________ __________________ (lose) the tennis match.

c) Emma is fond ________ __________________ (play) the piano.

d) Darren is good ________ __________________ (swim).

e) Martin is used ________ __________________ (work) hard.

f) Rebecca is interested ______ ______________ (earn) some pocket money.

g) Most pupils are tired _______ _______________ (learn) English grammar.

h) Stuart is crazy _______ _______________ (dance).

Das Gerund kann auch nach manchen **Adjektiven + Präposition** stehen, z. B. *proud* + *of* + ing-Form. Auch hier solltest du die Präpositionen, mit denen die Adjektive zusammengehen, kennen.

5. Complete: noun (+ preposition) + gerund.

a) Tom likes to sleep long; he often has trouble _______________________ (catch) his bus.

b) Jane didn't feel good; she had no chance _______________________ (win) her tennis match.

c) Mr Parker is a mechanic; he had no difficulty _______________________ (sell) his car.

d) The bell rang; there was no time _______________________ (finish) the exercise.

e) The bus arrived in time, so there was no reason _______________________ (be) late.

f) What is the advantage _______________________ (use) this PC?

g) I'm sorry, I had no intention _______________________ (push) you.

h) Susan isn't at home, so there's no point _______________________ (visit) her.

Das Gerund kann nach bestimmten **Substantiven + Präposition** folgen, z. B. *chance* + *of* + ing-Form. Es kann auch direkt auf manche Substantive folgen, z. B. *trouble* + ing-Form.

6. Translate into German.

a) You can improve your English by learning more effectively.

b) You can't become a good football player without practising a lot.

c) The boys were angry after losing the game.

d) You should concentrate instead of chattering all the time.

e) They tidied their desks before leaving the room.

f) They began to laugh on hearing the news.

Das Gerund folgt hier auf **allein stehende Präpositionen**, z. B. *instead of* – anstatt. Ein wörtliches Übersetzen ist oft nicht möglich, z. B. *You can improve ... by learning.* – Du kannst ... verbessern, indem du lernst.

Infinitiv mit *to* – Infinitiv ohne *to*

7. Fill in the infinitive without **to** or the "to-infinitive".

a) Paul can ________________ (play) tennis quite well.

b) He will be able ________________ (join) the local team next season.

c) The guard let Susan ________________ (enter) the hall.

d) He didn't allow all visitors ________________ (enter) at one time.

e) If you want ________________ (do) the whole exercise you should ________________ (start) now.

f) We could __________________ (go) to a disco if you don't want __________________ (stay) at home.

g) We ought __________________ (take) a key with us, then we can __________________ (return) late.

h) Would you like __________________ (have) this pen or shall I __________________ (show) you another one?

8. Translate into English.

a) Die Mädchen beschlossen, sich nächsten Samstag zu treffen.

____

b) Helen möchte ihren deutschen Brieffreund besuchen.

____

c) Wir mussten gestern zu Fuß nach Hause gehen.

____

d) Wir brauchen am Samstag nicht in die Schule zu gehen.

____

e) Peter ist krank; es wäre besser, wenn er den Arzt anruft.

____

f) Früher lebte Ellen bei ihren Eltern; heute hat sie eine eigene Wohnung.

____

Infinitiv ohne *to*: nach fast allen Hilfsverben (z. B. *I can go*) und *had better* (z. B. *You had better go*). **Infinitiv mit *to*:** nach *ought* (z. B. *I ought to go*) und *used to* (z. B. *He used to play*) und zahlreichen Verben (z. B. *want, decide*).

Infinitiv zur Satzverkürzung

9. Complete. Use an infinitive after the verb and object.

a) Karen can't sleep long. Mother wants ______________ ______________ (she, get up) before 7 o'clock.

b) Jane is my best friend. She taught ______________ ______________ (I, use) the Internet.

c) Helen must be punctual. We expect ______________ ______________ (she, be) on time.

d) I forgot about the money. Tina reminded ______________ ______________ (I, give) her the £100 back.

e) The girls were too loud. The teacher asked ______________ ______________ (they, be) quiet.

f) Peter was careless. His parents would like ______________ ______________ (he, be) more careful in future.

g) The boys hesitated. Their teacher encouraged ______________________________ (they, have) a try.

10. Translate into English.

a) Darren bat seine Schwester, ruhig zu sein.

____

b) Er erwartete, dass sie ihn nicht bei den Hausaufgaben störte.

____

c) Später sagte er: „Ich will, dass du mir hilfst."

____

d) Sie fragte: „Möchtest du, dass ich den Text abschreibe?"

____

e) Sie gab ihm den Rat, die Vokabeln zu wiederholen.

____

f) Dann fragte sie: „Willst du, dass wir den Text zusammen lesen?"

____

Der **Infinitiv mit *to*** steht nach bestimmten **Verben + Objekt**, z. B. *want* – wollen, dass; oder *would like* – möchte(n), dass. Mit dieser Satzkonstruktion vermeidest du Nebensätze im Englischen: *I want him to go.* – Ich will, dass er geht.

11. Rewrite the sentences using a construction with **for**.

a) Children should not smoke. It isn't good.

It isn't good ______________________________

b) You should go home now, Andrew. It's time.

It's time ______________________________

c) He isn't coming. Don't wait.

Don't wait ______________________________

d) This bag is too heavy for Susan. She can't carry it.

This bag is too heavy ______________________________

e) Patrick learned a lot. It was important for him.

It was ______________________________ *a lot.*

12. Translate into German.

a) It is important for young people to study foreign languages.

____

b) The weather was too bad for the plane to take off.

____

c) Please don't wait for me to be back for dinner.

____

d) There was no time for us to see the film. We had to leave.

____

e) Is it all right for me to stay?

____

Der **Infinitiv mit *to*** kann nach einigen Verben / Adjektiven / Substantiven + *for* + Substantiv / Pronomen stehen, z. B. *wait for* – warten auf, *important for* – wichtig für, *time for* – Zeit für / um zu. Ein wörtliches Übersetzen ist meist nicht möglich; oft hilft ein Nebensatz mit „dass", z. B. *they were waiting for him to come* – sie warteten darauf, dass er kommt.

13. Use the infinitive.

a) Can you tell me how I can get to the station?

Can you tell me ____________________ *to the station?*

b) Peter doesn't know what he could do in such a situation.

Peter doesn't know ____________________ *in such a situation.*

c) Emely wasn't sure where she could put the umbrella.

Emily wasn't sure ____________________ *the umbrella.*

d) The first person who arrived was John and the last one who left was his brother.

The first person ____________________ *was John and the last one*

____________________ *was his brother.*

e) The most popular group that sang at the concert was XXL.

The most popular group ____________________ *at the*

concert was XXL. ____________________

14. **Translate into German.**

a) James didn't know which way to go. He had lost his map.

____

b) He asked a policeman for help. This was the best thing to do.

____

c) The policeman told him where to go.

____

d) Helen had no idea how to prepare for the interview.

____

e) She had also forgotten where to go.

____

Der **Infinitiv mit *to*** kann nach **Fragewörtern** einen abhängigen Fragesatz ersetzen, z. B. *(I don't know) how I can get* ➧ *... how to get*. Er steht anstelle eines Relativsatzes nach **Superlativen oder Zahlwörtern**, z. B. *the most popular group that sang* ➧ *the most popular group to sing.*

Vermischte Übungen

15. **Fill in the correct forms of the verbs in brackets.**

Here is a report about some of Martin's friends.

a) Darren enjoys ______________ (fly) in a plane. He likes ______________ (travel) by air because it is exciting for him. He would like ______________ (see) New York in his holidays.

b) Lucy, however, prefers ______________ (go) by train to ______________ (fly). She wants ______________ (visit) Paris in August. She hopes ______________ (be) able to improve her French.

c) David doesn't like ____________________ (go) away at all. So he decided ____________________ (stay) at home in his last holidays. This year he is planning ____________________ (build) a wooden hut in the garden. He says: "I enjoy ____________________ (do) practical work."

d) Rebecca has given up ____________________ (smoke). She used ____________________ (smoke) over twenty cigarettes a day. She says: "I can't go on ____________________ (ruin) my health. I hope ____________________ (be) strong enough."

e) Simon is a computer freak. He is used ____________________ (sit) in front of his computer for hours on end. He never has time ____________________ (go) out, and his friends have given up ____________________ (ask) him to come with them.

f) Stuart has decided ____________________ (learn) Italian. He wants ____________________ (visit) Rome next summer and he is looking forward ____________________ (talk) to lots of Italian girls.

Überlege: Infinitiv, Gerund oder Präposition + Gerund?
Halte auseinander:

He used to go …	Früher ging er … und
He is used to going …	Er ist es gewöhnt, … zu gehen

16. Ask your penfriend about his / her hobbies.

Du willst wissen, ob er / sie …

a) … gern Tennis spielt;

____

b) … auch nicht gern in die Disco geht;

____

c) … daran interessiert ist, an einem Sommerlager teilzunehmen;

____

d) … im Schwimmen gut ist;

____

e) … an den Meisterschaften teilnehmen will;

____

f) … sich freut dich bald zu sehen.

____

17. Guided Writing.

You are asked to enquire about holiday apartments in Derbyshire. Use: **want, would like, look forward.**

a) Du möchtest weitere Informationen bekommen.

I ____

b) Du willst eine Ferienwohnung buchen.

I ____

c) Deine Eltern möchten den Preis für vier Personen erfahren.

My ____

d) Du freust dich auf eine baldige Antwort.

I ____

18. Give your opinion.

Do you like living in your home town? Give three reasons why / why not.

____

____

____

19. Translate into German.

a) Darren can't give up smoking.

b) Julie is interested in meeting nice people.

c) Petra passed the test by studying very hard.

d) These records aren't worth buying.

e) How about having some coffee?

f) It's no use waiting any longer.

g) Grandfather used to live in an old country cottage.

h) Craig is likely to be the winner.

i) Stuart likes playing the keyboard.

j) Jonathan dislikes getting up early.

Übe **freies Übersetzen**, z. B. a) … das Rauchen aufgeben, b) … ist daran interessiert, c) … , indem sie tüchtig lernte, d) Es lohnt sich nicht, … h) wird wahrscheinlich … sein, i) … spielt gern, j) … steht ungern auf.

Prüfungsaufgaben

20. Give an example each for "he used to, I am used to, to use for" and "it's no use" to show the difference in meaning. You may use the following words: **smoke – get up early – tool – wait.**

a) ______________________________ (1/1)

b) ______________________________ (1/1)

c) ______________________________ (1/1)

d) ______________________________ (1/1)

21. Complete the following text.

Craig Kielburger from Canada is only 12, and already has got a mission. He runs a group which is called "Free the Children". The organisation is trying a) ______________ (influence) governments b) ______________ (stop) child labour. Craig started the group after c) ______________ (read) about a 12-year-old Pakistani boy who had been murdered because he had spoken out against exploitation of children. Craig has already been to Geneva d) ______________ (talk) to experts about the problem. These people have great difficulties e) ______________ (listen) to him because he is so young. Next month he will fly to Asia. He wants f) ______________ (support) child workers in North Pakistan. (6)

22. Answer in complete sentences.

What are your favourite hobbies? Name two and give two reasons why you like them. You may use these words: I like …, I'm fond of …, … is my hobby. (2/4)

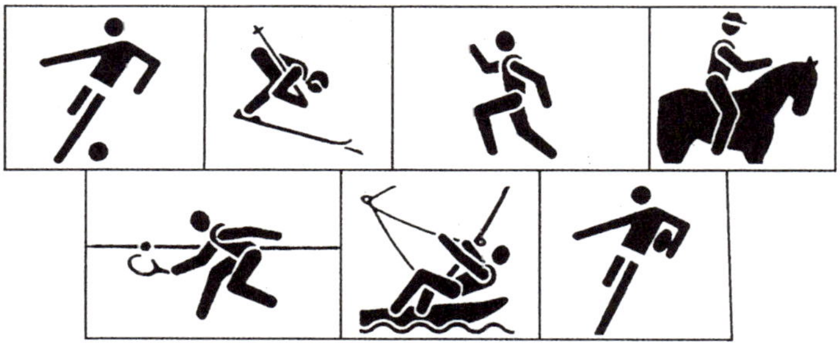

23. Say whether you agree or disagree with the following statements and say why.

a) Earning money while going to school makes you independent from your parents. (2/2)

b) Having a job and going to school don't fit together. (2/2)

24. Greenwich – the centre of space and time. Translate into German.

a) Two of the great puzzles throughout the centuries were how to find your way across the seas and how to tell the exact time. (3)

b) After working in his observatory for forty-three years the royal astronomer John Flamsteed established the Greenwich Meridian in 1676. (3)

c) This enabled each captain to know the exact position of his ship. (2)

d) In 1884 it was decided to set all clocks according to Greenwich time. (2)

25. **Underline the four mistakes and correct them.** (4)

a) Susan enjoys to play tennis in winter.

b) Paul is used to get up early.

c) Simon has decided to come earlier.

d) Ian wants that his friends help him.

e) Paul is looking forward to see Helen.

I If-Sätze

If-Sätze vom Typ 1

1. Complete the sentences.

a) If you do this exercise carefully, you ____________________ (understand) it.

b) Gary will pass his exam if he ____________________ (work) hard.

c) You can't succeed if you ____________________ (not, try).

d) What ____________________ (you, do) if you fail the exam?

e) If Emma comes home late, her mother ____________________ (be angry).

Im **if-Satz Typ 1** steht das Verb im ***present*** (z. B. *do, doesn't work*), im **Hauptsatz** steht ***will*** (z. B. *will understand*). Anstelle von *will* kann ein anderes **Modalverb** (z. B. *can, must*) verwendet werden.

2. Form sentences with if-clause type 1.

Emma is telling her friend Rosie about her plans for her next holidays.

a) the weather good / stay at the seaside

____

b) go by car / certainly visit the Lake District

____

c) find a nice place / go camping

____

d) need a bigger tent / my friends come with me

____

e) there is a chance / take a boat trip on the canal

f) have a look round / pass a pretty village

g) have time / go to lovely pubs in the evenings

h) put on waterproof clothing / rain

i) take photos / send you some

Vor *if* steht kein **Komma**. Beginnt der Satz mit *if*, dann setzt du ein Komma vor den Hauptsatz.

3. Give answers to these questions.

a) What will you do if you pass your exam? – (go on holiday)

b) What will you do if you have a lot of time? – (sleep longer in the morning)

c) What will you do if your friends give a big party? – (try to get invited)

d) Where will you go if you visit the USA? – (New York and the Rocky Mountains)

e) When will you phone me if you are at home? – (at 7 o'clock)

____

____

If-Sätze vom Typ 2

4. Complete the sentences.

a) They would buy new shoes if they ____________ (have) the opportunity.

b) Gary ____________ (not, ask) if he knew the answer.

c) Emma wouldn't be so good at running if she ____________ (not, train) so much.

d) What ____________ (can do, your friend) if he came to visit you?

e) If you ____________ (be) older, you would get a job in your holidays.

Im **if-Satz Typ 2** steht das Verb im ***past*** (z. B. *had*), im **Hauptsatz** steht ***would*** (z. B. *would buy*). Anstelle von *would* kann ein anderes **Modalverb** (z. B. *could, might*) verwendet werden.

5. Form sentences with if-clause type 2.

Rosie is telling her friend Craig what she would like to do.

a) win a lot of money on the lottery / travel round the world

____

____

b) travel round the world / see a lot of interesting countries

____

____

c) have a chance / first fly to New York

____

____

d) be in New York / try to get tickets for the Metropolitan Opera

____

____

e) go to the Metropolitan Opera / meet many nice people

____

____

f) talk to many Americans / improve my knowledge of English

____

____

6. Answer the following questions in English.

a) Was würdest du tun, wenn du viel Geld hättest? – **(travel to New York)**

If I ______________________________________

____

b) Was würdest du tun, wenn du in New York wärst? – **(take a lot of photographs)**

____

____

c) Was könntest du sehen, wenn du in Manhattan wärst? – **(many skyscrapers)**

____

____

If-Sätze vom Typ 3

7. Complete the sentences.

a) If I had known the answer, I ______________________ (tell) you.

b) What would your friend have said if you ______________________ (not, come) in time.

c) If you had been ready, you ______________________ (can, come) with me.

d) Tom ______________________ (not, be) so sad if his girlfriend had danced with him.

e) If Angela ______________________ (not, work) so hard, she would not have succeeded.

Im **if-Satz Typ 3** steht das Verb im ***past perfect*** (z. B. *had known*), im **Hauptsatz** steht ***would have + past participle*** (z. B. *would have told*). Anstelle von *would* kann ein anderes **Modalverb** (z. B. *could, might*) verwendet werden.

8. Form sentences with if-clause type 3.

Craig is telling his friend Gary about his last holidays.

a) save more money / spend more time in Ireland

____

____

b) get better information / read books about that country

____

____

c) have better information / visit more interesting places

____

____

d) have the chance / take my car with me

___

___

e) take my car / see more of the countryside

___

___

f) the weather be not so bad / go to one of the islands

___

___

g) find one of the "singing pubs" / spend an evening there

___

___

9. Answer the following questions in English. Use if-clauses.

a) Was hättest du getan, wenn du in den Ferien mehr Zeit gehabt hättest? – (travel to Ireland)

If I ___

___

b) Wo hätte Craig Rosie treffen können, wenn er in der Stadt gewesen wäre? – (in the cafe)

___

___

c) Wohin wären sie gegangen, wenn sie sich getroffen hätten? – (to the cinema)

___

___

Vermischte Übungen

10. Complete the sentences.

Plans for a holiday

Emma: What will you do if you ________________ (travel) to England next month, Craig?

Craig: If my friend agrees, we ________________ (visit) London. I ________________ (take) my camera, in case we ________________ (go) to the Tower.

Rosie: Where would you go if you ________________ (have) enough money for a long holiday, Holly?

Holly: Well, if I had enough money, I ________________ (fly) to New York. If I ________________ (be) you, I certainly ________________ (stay) there for 3 months.

Joe: What would you have done if you ________________ (be) in London last winter James?

James: If I had been there, I ________________ (try) to get tickets for a musical. My friend ________________ with me if I ________________ (invite) him.

in case = falls, wenn

11. Complete the following dialogue using the right tense of the verbs in brackets.

Going to Scotland

Kirsty: If I can persuade my father, we certainly ________________ (travel) to the Highlands this year.

Adam: Unless you have seen Edinburgh, you ________________ (cannot say) that you know Scotland.

Kirsty: Have you made up your mind yet, whether you ________________ (come) on holiday with us?

Adam: No, not yet, because my father ________________ (only give) me the money for the journey if I ________________ (pass) my exams in May.

Kirsty: I think, you could easily succeed if you ________________ (learn) a little more. If I ________________ (be) you, I ________________ (pay) more attention at school. You could be more successful at school, if you ________________ (not spend) all your time on the tennis court.

Adam: And I ________________ (be glad) if you ________________ (not remind) me of that all the time.

unless = if not; whether = if

12. Say it in English.

a) Craig fragt seine Freundin Rosie, was sie tun würde, wenn sie genug Geld hätte.

____

b) Rosie antwortet, dass sie, wenn sie so viel Geld hätte wie er, jedes Jahr zweimal Urlaub machen würde.

____

____

c) Craig sagt, dass
sie zusammen fahren können, wenn sie ihren Urlaub im Juli nimmt.

d) Rosie sagt, dass sie,
wenn sie durch England reisen, ihre Freunde in Durham besuchen werden.

e) Craig sagt, dass sie,
wenn sie die Möglichkeit hätten, ihre Fahrräder mitnehmen könnten.

Prüfungsaufgaben

13. **If-clauses. Write down the correct form of the verbs.**

a) (attend) If the Donaldsons didn't live on Montague Island, Michael ______ primary school. (1)

b) (disturb) You ______ the rare seabirds if you don't move about quietly on the island. (1)

c) (not be) If the island ______ a nature reserve, many more tourists would visit it. (1)

14. **Complete the following sentences. Use the correct form of the words in brackets.**

a) If he had known me better, he ______ (react) differently. (1)

b) Maybe he would be more successful if he ______ (be) older. (1)

c) If she ______________________________ (try) a particularly complicated question, would the computer still understand her? (1)

d) If an extremely fast spaceship ______________________________ (start) out ten thousand years ago, it ____________________________________ (cover) only six per cent of the distance of a lightyear till now. (2)

e) But if there ______________________ (be) enough lifeboats on the Titanic, many more ____ (escape) the disaster. (2)

15. Questions on the text.

a) If you had the chance to change or stay at the same school? What would you do? Give reason for your answer. – (stay there, don't like to leave my friends) (1/3)

____

____

b) If you were in London, what means of transport would you use? Give one reason for your answer. – (go by bus / see more) (1/2)

____

____

c) If you were offered the chance to go to school in New York for a year, would you accept? Give three reasons for your answer. (not / not good at English; parents not let me go / not the money / afraid of high crime rate) (3/3/1)

____

____

____

____

____

16. What would you do if …?

Say **what** you would do in the situations mentioned below and say **why** you would do so. Choose **two** situations and write about **25 words** each.

a) You get the news that you have won first prize in a competition.
b) A cyclist has knocked you over as you walked home from school.
c) The police stop you on your motorbike because your passenger wasn't wearing a helmet.
d) You are at a fair and you see a child who has lost his parents.

(6)

17. Underline the four mistakes and correct them. (4)

a) Mr Brown would help you if you would ask him. (Herr Brown würde dir helfen, wenn du ihn fragen würdest.)

b) I don't speak to you again if you don't apologize. (Ich spreche nicht wieder mit dir, wenn du dich nicht entschuldigst.)

c) What would you have done if you have been in England last summer? (Was hättest du getan, wenn du letzten Sommer in England gewesen wärst?)

d) If I go on holiday, I travel to Scotland. (Falls ich Ferien mache, reise ich nach Schottland.)

J Indirekte Rede

Reporting verb (= einleitendes Verb) im *present / present perfect*

1. Put into reported speech.

a) Mrs Nolan says, "I want a bigger house."

____

b) Sam adds, "I need a room of my own."

____

c) The children ask, "Where are we moving to?"

____

d) Mr Nolan remarks, "I guess we'll have to look for a larger place."

____

____

e) Mrs Nolan has always said, "We must have a house with six rooms."

____

____

f) Judy says, "I'm old enough to have a room of my own."

____

____

g) Mrs Nolan wants to know, "Are we going to buy a new house?"

____

____

Wenn das *reporting verb* im ***present*** oder ***present perfect*** steht, bleiben die Zeitformen gleich. Die **Pronomen** werden sinngemäß **verändert**. Bei der indirekten Frage übernimmst du das Fragewort der direkten Rede. **Indirekte Yes / No-Fragen** werden mit ***if*** oder ***whether*** gebildet. Beachte hier die normale **Wortstellung** (S – V – O)!

Reporting verb im *past / past perfect*

2. Put into reported speech.

a) Mr Nolan asked, "Do we want a bigger house?"

____

b) Mrs Nolan answered, "It is absolutely necessary for us to have six rooms."

____

____

c) Sam added, "I saw an advertisement in the newspaper."

____

d) Judy had said, "I've always wanted a room of my own."

____

e) She declared, "And I like to have a room with a large window."

____

____

f) Sam wanted to know, "When do we buy a new house?"

____

g) Mrs Nolan remarked, "I think the estate agent has got many houses for sale."

____

____

Steht das ***reporting verb*** im ***past*** oder ***past perfect***, verändern sich neben den **Pronomen** auch die **Zeitformen**: *present* ➧ *past; past* ➧ *past / past perfect; present perfect* ➧ *past perfect; future* ➧ *conditional; future perfect* ➧ *conditional perfect.*

Veränderungen der Modalverben

3. Put into reported speech.

a) Mr Nolan said, "We'll buy a new house if the bank gives us the money."

b) Judy asked, "What will we do with the old one?"

c) Her father replied, "I'll go to the estate agent's and try to sell it."

d) Mrs Nolan remarked, "We must get a good price for the old house."

e) Her husband said, "You needn't worry. I can easily find a buyer."

f) Sam asked, "May I have a room upstairs?"

g) His father answered, "You must wait until we've got an offer."

h) Mrs Nolan added, "If it's possible, each of us will get his own room."

Die **Modalverben** verändern sich wie folgt: *will* ➧ *would; may* ➧ *might; must* ➧ *had to; needn't* ➧ *didn't have to; can* ➧ *could*. *Could, should, would, might* werden **nicht verändert**.

Weitere Veränderungen

4. **Put into reported speech.**

a) Mrs Nolan said, "I don't like this place any more."

____

b) She added, "We were reading all these advertisements."

____

c) Her husband mentioned, "I don't like it here either."

____

d) Then he added, "I'll have a look at the newspaper today."

____

e) Sam said, "My friend showed me his room yesterday."

____

____

f) Grandma declared, "I'll move out tomorrow."

____

g) Father replied, „We'll have a larger house next week."

____

____

h) "Last month you just said the same", said grandmother.

____

____

i) Mrs Nolan said, "We missed a good chance a year ago."

____

____

Weitere Veränderungen bei der Umwandlung von direkter in indirekte Rede: *this* ➧ *that; these* ➧ *those; today* ➧ *that day; yesterday* ➧ *the day before; tomorrow* ➧ *the next / the following day; last month* ➧ *the previous month; a year ago* ➧ *a year before*.

Befehl und Bitte

5. **Put into reported speech.**

a) Mrs Nolan said to Sam: "Listen to me."

b) Judy said: "Please leave me alone, Sam."

c) Sam shouted: "Don't lose your temper."

d) Judy replied: "Don't make such a fuss about everything."

e) Mrs Nolan said: "Can you speak about that problem with your father, Judy?"

f) Father said: "Stop quarrelling."

g) Mrs Nolan said to Sam: "When you've finished, go upstairs."

h) She added: "Switch the lights off before you go to bed, Judy."

Einen **Befehl** drückst du mit ***tell*** **+ Objekt + to-Infinitiv** aus (z. B. *She told Sam …*). Über eine **Bitte** berichtest du mit ***ask*** **+ Objekt + to-Infinitiv** (z. B. *She asked her to …*).

Vermischte Übungen

6. Put the following dialogue between Sam and Judy into reported speech.

Judy: "Do you know that Mum is looking for a new house?"

a) Judy asked Sam

Sam: "I heard her talking about this matter yesterday."

b)

Judy: "Do you want to move?"

c)

Sam: "No, I don't want to leave here."

d)

Judy: "Do you know how much a new house will cost?"

e)

Sam: "No, I don't; but I don't think that we can afford to buy a new one."

f)

Judy: "If we voted against this plan, Mum and Dad couldn't refuse our proposals."

g)

Sam: "What are you going to propose?"

h)

Judy: "We could convert the attic into a big room."

i)

Sam: "Oh! That's wonderful. I will tell Steve immediately."

j) ______________________________

____

7. Mrs Nolan tells her husband what the estate agent told her on the phone.

Agent: "My name is Bardon. I spoke to your husband about an offer last week. He asked me if I could find a suitable house for him. I've got a wonderful place which I'm sure will be large enough for your family. Can you talk about it with your family? Please let me know when you've made up your mind to move into this lovely home."

Mrs Nolan:

"Yesterday the estate agent phoned me that ______________________________

______________________________"

Versetze dich in Mrs Nolan, die ihrem Mann erzählt, was der Makler ihr am Telefon gesagt hat. Denke an die Veränderungen, die du vornehmen musst (z. B. Zeitformen, Pronomen, Adverbien).

8. Put the following conversation into English. Use direct speech.

a) Mr Nolan sagte, dass er ein neues Haus kaufen möchte.

Mr Nolan:

"____

____"

b) Die Kinder bemerkten, dass sie sehr glücklich seien, wenn jedes ein eigenes Zimmer haben würde.

The children:

"____

____"

c) Sam fragte, ob er ein Zimmer im ersten Stock haben könnte.

Sam:

"____

____?"

d) Seine Mutter antwortete, dass es darauf ankomme, wie viele Zimmer sie haben würden.

Mother:

"____

____"

e) Judy fragte, wie viel ein neues Haus kosten würde.

Judy:

"____

____"

f) Ihr Vater antwortete, dass sie viel Geld sparen müssten, aber er denke, dass sie es bis nächstes Jahr geschafft haben würden.

Father:

"____

____

____"

g) Mrs Nolan fügte hinzu, dass alle helfen sollten.

Mrs Nolan:

"____"

Das Gespräch wird in direkter Rede wiedergegeben. Beachte dabei, dass du nicht immer wörtlich übersetzen kannst.

Prüfungsaufgaben

9. Interpreting

You are staying at a hotel near Yosemite National Park. At the reception desk, Herr Schmid, a tourist from Germany, is trying to get some information about national parks. He does not speak English very well and asks you to do the interpreting for him.

Herr Schmid: „Ich möchte morgen den Yosemite Nationalpark besuchen und möchte gern wissen, wie ich am besten dort hinkommen kann."

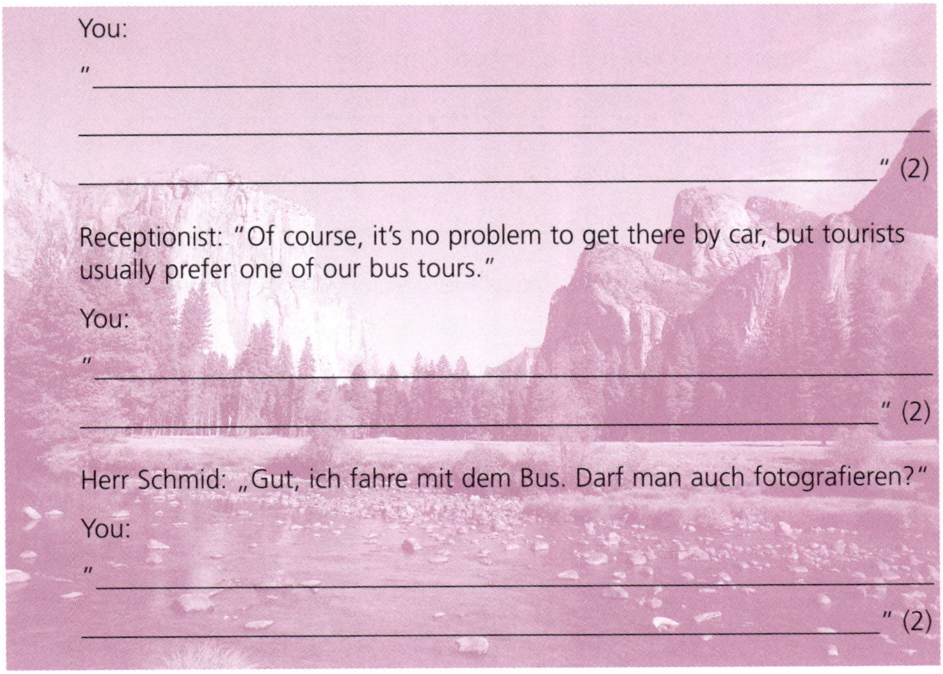

You:

"____

____

____" (2)

Receptionist: "Of course, it's no problem to get there by car, but tourists usually prefer one of our bus tours."

You:

"____

____" (2)

Herr Schmid: „Gut, ich fahre mit dem Bus. Darf man auch fotografieren?"

You:

"____

____" (2)

Receptionist: "There will be stops at the most spectacular places of interest. Your guide will give you time enough to walk around and enjoy the scenery."

You:

"____

____

____" (2)

Herr Schmid: „Vielen Dank für ihre Hilfe. Auf Wiedersehen."

You:

"____" (2)

10. Underline the five mistakes and correct them. (5)

a) Mrs Brown asked me where I am going.

____

b) Mr Brown asked where had his wife gone.

____

c) Mrs Baker says Tom to get up earlier.

____

d) The teacher told the boys to don't talk so loud.

____

e) Mr Brown wanted to know why his wife had not come earlier.

____

f) Mrs Brown said that she should travel to Italy next year.

____

g) Tom asked them where they could spend the weekend.

____

K Partizipialsätze

Partizipien in Relativsätzen

1. Replace the relative clause with the participle.

a) The train which leaves at 8 o'clock goes to Glasgow.

____

b) The man who is knocking at the door is a milkman.

____

c) The street which leads to the castle is very narrow.

____

d) In our town there is a lot of pollution which is caused by too much traffic.

____

e) Do you know the girl who is talking to Darren?

____

f) Films which were made in Hollywood are very popular in Europe.

____

Mit Partizipien kannst du **Relativsätze** *(relative clauses)* **verkürzen** (z. B. *The train which leaves ...* ➧ *The train leaving ...*).

Partizipien in Nebensätzen des Grundes

2. Use particples for the clauses of reason.

a) As Darren was tired, he went to bed early.

______________________________, Darren went to bed early.

b) Because she felt frightened, Emma stayed at home.

______________________________, Emma stayed at home.

c) As Jennifer wanted to catch the last bus, she had to leave on time.

______________________ the last bus, Jennifer had to leave on time.

d) Simon could not show his identity card as he had lost his wallet.

Simon could not show his identity card __________________________.

e) As Katie didn't know the way, she had to ask a policeman.

__________________________, Katie had to ask a policeman.

f) As he was injured, James could not take part in the cycling tour.

__________________________, James could not take part in the cycling tour.

Mit Partizipien kannst du **Nebensätze des Grundes** *(clauses of reason)* **verkürzen**: *As* bzw. *because* = weil, da, fallen dabei weg. Beachte die veränderte Stellung des Namens im Hauptsatz: *As Darren was tired, he … ➧ … tired, Darren …*

Partizipien in Nebensätzen der Zeit

3. Change the sentences using participles.

a) While I was walking in the park, I met Rachel.

____

b) Before you hand in your report you should read it again.

____

c) When Lucy heard the telephone she stopped working.

____

d) After Andrew had helped his mother, he cycled to his friends.

____

e) You must be very careful when you cross the street.

____

f) When Mr Winter saw the taxi he stopped it at once.

____

Mit Partizipien kannst du **Nebensätze der Zeit** *(clauses of time)* **verkürzen**. Die Konjunktionen *while* – während, *when* – als und *after* – nachdem, können weggelassen werden. Beachte die veränderte Stellung des Namens im Hauptsatz: *After Andrew had helped his mother, he cycled …*
➧ *After … , Andrew cycled …*

Partizipien zur Verbindung von Hauptsätzen

4. **Make one sentence out of two. Use a participle.**

a) Sheila walked down the lane. She sang.

____

b) Darren and Helen were in the kitchen. They washed the dishes.

____

c) Mr Miller sat in his armchair. He smoked his pipe.

____

d) Craig went to bed. He hoped to fall asleep immediately.

____

e) Karen picked up the telephone and looked forward to hearing her mother's voice.

____

Mit Partizipien kannst du **zwei Hauptsätze zusammenfügen**. Wenn es sich in beiden Sätzen um das gleiche Subjekt handelt, kann das Personalpronomen wegfallen.

Partizip Präsens oder Partizip Perfekt?

5. Fill in: present participle or past participle?

a) The old lady ____________________ (live) next door is 92 years old.

b) ______________ (feel) he was right Peter protested against the decision.

c) The articles ____________________ (sell) in the supermarket are cheap.

d) Spanish is the language __________________ (speak) in most countries in South America.

e) We met a group of girls ________________ (travel) to France.

f) The number of people ________________ (injure) in the accident is low.

Das ***present participle*** – Partizip Präsens – hat immer **aktivische Bedeutung** (z. B. *the old lady living …* – die alte Dame, die … wohnt), das ***past participle*** – Partizip Perfekt – immer **passivische Bedeutung** (z. B. *The articles sold …* – die Artikel, die … verkauft werden).

Vermischte Übungen

6. Write the sentences with a relative pronoun.

a) People driving to work every day are called commuters.

____

b) The girl sitting on the bench is Kathy.

____

c) The car stopped by the police belongs to Fred.

____

d) Trains going to Glasgow leave from platform 4.

____

e) The flag flying on the roof is the Union Jack.

____

f) Books bought at a flea market are cheap.

____

7. Rewrite these sentences. Begin with **as / because, when** or **while**.

a) Wanting to get home as soon as possible we hitch-hiked.

____

b) Not knowing the language, Darren was helpless in France.

____

c) Seeing the old man beside the road, the driver slowed down.

____

d) Listening to Helen's story, the boys got very excited.

____

e) Coming into the room, Jonathan heard the phone.

____

f) Sitting in the pub, we could see the trains go by.

____

8. Translate into German.

a) Being tired, Helen sat down for a while.

____

b) Peter sat on his couch reading a book.

____

c) Matthew walked down the road, whistling.

____

d) Being lonely herself, Jane understood Helen's problem.

____

e) People wishing to visit the museum must ring the doorbell.

f) Convinced that he was right, George didn't give in.

g) Feeling very tired, Geoff went straight to bed.

h) Not wanting to lose the football match, Patrick and his friends trained three times last week.

i) A car bought ten years ago isn't worth much today.

j) The day being fine, the children decided to play in the garden.

Überlege dir die **Bedeutung** des verkürzten Satzes: Ist es ein Relativsatz (… , der / die / das), ein Nebensatz des Grundes (… , da / weil), ein Nebensatz der Zeit (als / während) oder eine Satzverknüpfung (… und …)?

Prüfungsaufgaben

9. Complete the following text. Use the correct form of the words in brackets. (8)

Dog Steals Car

A dog a) ______________________ (call) Mick was arrested in the Oxford district yesterday for stealing a car. Mrs Johnson was driving from Northampton to Oxford to visit her sister, when she noticed a big, sorrowful dog at the side of the road. b) ______________________ (think) that the dog might have been lost she stopped the car and, c) ______________________ (leave) the door open, rushed to help the poor animal. As she approached, the dog suddenly leapt up and, d) ______________________ (rush) past her it jumped up onto the driver's seat e) ______________________ (put) its front paws on the steering wheel. The lady tried without success to persuade the dog to get out of the seat. f) ______________________ (resist) all her attempts it just sat there g) ______________________ (snap) whenever she got too close. Finally, h) ______________________ (realise) that the dog was not willing to surrender Mrs Johnson used her mobile phone to ring Oxford police station with her incredible story.

10. Make one sentence out of two and write it down. Use ing-forms.

a) Senior citizens feel stronger and more energetic these days. They don't want to give up their jobs. (1)

____

____

b) A lot of American teenagers work for money. They are less dependent on their parents. (1)

____

____

11. Translate into German.

a) 15-year-old Eni paints the soles of sports shoes, sweating in terrible heat. (3)

____

b) The factory employs 13,000 people wearing cheap plastic shoes because none of them can afford the shoes they make. (4)

____

____

c) Eni is paid 25 cents an hour. Compared to this, a pair of tennis shoes costs about $150. (2)

____

____

d) There are a lot of accidents caused by old machines. (2)

____

____

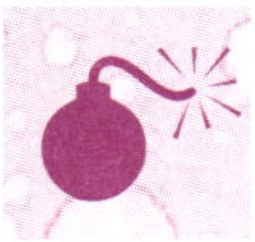

12. Underline the three mistakes and correct them. (3)

a) The film which made in France is fantastic.

____

b) When visiting Julie, Peter wore his best suit.

____

c) As being cold we put on our coats.

____

d) There was complete silence breaking only by a train.

____

L *Wortstellung*

Einfacher Aussagesatz

1. Make sentences.

a) plays / the / Ian / guitar

____

b) Jane / her / doing / homework / is

____

c) Russian / can / Ian / speak

____

d) a dog / has / and / Mary / got / a cat

____

Adverb der Häufigkeit

2. Make sentences.

a) the / swimming / boys / seldom / go

____

b) never / drank / Susan / coffee

____

c) together / Susan / do / and / their / Jill / homework / always

____

d) the / Mr Miller / finish / usually / can / crossword puzzle

____

Das **Adverb der Häufigkeit** steht vor dem Vollverb, hinter dem Hilfsverb und hinter einer Form von *to be*.

Adverbien des Ortes und der Zeit

3. Make sentences.

a) Mr Talbot works. – (at the weekend, often, in the garden)

____

b) Tom eats. – (never, in the morning, cornflakes)

____

c) Jean likes to listen to music. – (in her room, in the evening, usually)

____

____

d) Mr Brown reads his newspaper. – (always, after breakfast, on Sunday)

____

____

e) Mr Brown makes tea. – (on Sunday morning, sometimes, in the kitchen)

____

____

Das **Adverb des Ortes** steht meist am Satzende, das **Adverb der Zeit** meist am Anfang oder Ende des Satzes. Die genauere Zeitangabe steht vor der allgemeineren *(after breakfast on Sunday).*

4. Say it in English.

a) Sage, dass dein Bruder immer mit dem Bus zur Schule fährt.

____

____

b) Sage, dass du am Samstag nie Schule hast.

____

c) Sage, dass du manchmal am Sonntag in der Küche Tee machst.

d) Sage, dass dein Freund oft am Nachmittag im Stadion Fußball spielt.

e) Sage, dass ihr im Sommer selten im Fluss zum Schwimmen geht.

f) Sage, dass eure Familie im Urlaub gewöhnlich zusammen Fahrrad fährt.

Adverb der Art und Weise – Gradadverb

5. Put the adverbs in the right place.

a) The incident happened. + on a platform in London + last night

b) A crowd of young people were behaving … + very + rudely

c) An old lady went up to the loudest youth. + slowly

d) She found his behaviour bad. + terribly

e) The other travellers read their papers. + quietly

f) They concentrated on their papers. + simply

g) It was surprising that they said nothing. + really

h) The old lady's reaction was right. + absolutely

i) The stationmaster could have told the youths to behave. + more politely

Das **Adverb der Art und Weise** steht meist am Satzende (nach dem Objekt, bzw. dem Verb). Das **Gradadverb** steht gewöhnlich vor dem Adjektiv bzw. dem Adverb, das es bestimmt.

Verben mit zwei Objekten

6. Answer the following questions.

a) What did Tom show the controller? – (his ticket)

b) What did Jane give her mother for her birthday? – (some beautiful flowers)

c) What does Mr Molyneux teach the pupils? – (French)

d) What does Mr Moneymaker promise his workers? – (higher wages)

e) Who did Sam send a letter to? – (Mary, not Jane)

____

____

f) Who does Tony lend £10 to? – (his friend, not his brother)

____

____

g) What will Mr Brown sell his uncle? – (his old car)

____

h) What does Mother tell her children? – (a nice story)

____

Nach einigen Verben können zwei Objekte stehen. Das **indirekte Objekt** steht gewöhnlich vor dem **direkten**. Willst du das indirekte Objekt betonen, dann steht es mit *to* am Satzende.

7. Finish the sentences.

a) Henry tried to describe ______________________________.
(the accident, policeman)

b) Sarah could not explain ______________________________.
(her father, the problem)

c) Mrs Taylor prefers ______________________________.
(tea, milk)

d) Mr Talbot introduced ______________________________.
(the landlady, himself)

e) The policeman added ______________________________.
(the report, another detail)

f) The pupils said ______________________________.
(the teacher, good morning)

Nach einigen Verben steht das **indirekte Objekt** immer mit *to* am Satzende.

Satzverbindungen mit Konjunktionen

8. Connect the sentences with the following conjunctions:
although (2 x), **after, because, before, but** (2 x), **when**.

a) Hundreds of fans had come to the airport. The plane landed.

b) The fans got extremely excited. The singers came in sight.

c) The singers wanted to go to their hotel. They had to sing a song first.

d) The guitarist didn't want to play. He was so tired.

e) Most of the fans bought tickets. They were very expensive.

f) The performance had already lasted for an hour. The crowd demanded more songs.

g) The crowd had asked for another song. The band began to play.

h) The crowd pushed forward. The police prevented them from getting through.

____

____

Vermischte Übungen

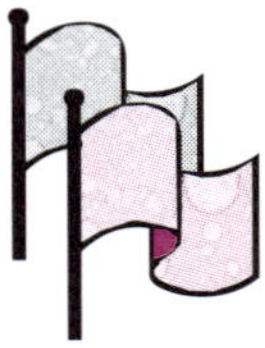

9. Make sentences with the correct word order.

a) Malta / in the south of Europe / is / a small island

____

b) the / and / Tower / are / in London / Buckingham Palace / sights

____

____

c) an / in / old / England / is / Eton / public school

____

d) between / autumn / winter / summer / is / the / season / and

____

e) when / you / birthday / the day / were / of the year / born / your / is

____

____

f) where / land / an airport / or / take off / a place / is / aeroplanes

____

g) music / composes / a / musician / or / a / instrument / plays / musical

____

h) is / a / school / live / boarding-school / pupils / where / a

____

10. Define the following words in complete sentences. Use the prompts.

a) The White House – (official residence / Washington/ US president)

b) a cruise liner – (large / comfortable ship / swimming pools / hundreds of waiters / plenty of food, drinks)

c) lifeboat – (on large ship / rescue passengers / ship in danger / sinking)

d) commercials – (advertisements / radio / television)

e) a holiday – (time / no school)

f) a crowd – (large number / people / together / join / place)

g) breakfast – (in the morning / first meal)

h) Denmark – (Northern Europe / small country)

i) a donkey – (animal / long ears / look / small horse)

j) a film library – (place / borrow / film)

Du musst hier Definitionen von Wörtern bilden. Verwende dafür die in Klammern angegebenen Hilfen.

Prüfungsaufgaben

11. Define the following words in complete sentences.

a) A debt: (1/2)

b) An expert: (1/2)

c) A dinosaur: (1/2)

d) A skyscraper: (1/2)

e) A burglar: (1/2)

f) A housewife: (1/2)

g) A computer freak: (1/2)

h) A manager: (1/2)

12. Questions on the text. Answer in complete sentences.

The Titanic disaster was caused by a combination of bad luck, poor planning and foolish decisions. Captain James Smith's most fateful decision was to ignore the seven ice warnings he had received on Sunday, 14 April. The great ship was travelling – at nearly full speed – across the Atlantic from Southampton to New York for the first time. Then, 400 miles south of Newfoundland, a member of the crew suddenly spotted an iceberg right ahead at 11.37 p.m. A few minutes later there was a strange noise. The huge iceberg hit the Titanic, the ship, which was thought to be unsinkable. The ship was designed to be the safest with its 16 watertight compartments. Up to four compartments could be flooded without any danger to the ship.

a) Where and when did the disaster happen? (1/1)

____

____

b) What made people believe that the Titanic was unsinkable? (1/1)

____

____

c) What should the captain have done to avoid the disaster? (1/1)

____

____

d) How did the people on board know that the iceberg had hit the ship? (1/1)

____

____

Additional Question

Why do many people like to spend their holidays on ships? Give two reasons in about two sentences. (2/2+1)

____

____

____

13. Letter writing

You have got a pen-friend in England and you would like to tell him / her about your holiday in Australia. Choose 5 items from the list below to write a letter of about 150 words. (20)

- natives
- food
- outback
- wildlife
- accommodation
- climate
- a beach party
- sights
- sports or other activities
- a picnic in a national park

30th April, ____________

Dear ______________________,

Guess where I am at the moment. ____________

____

____

____

____

____

____

____

____

____

____

Yours ______________________

14. Describe a person you know well. Refer to the points given below.

Please write about the teenager's …

- interests
- attitude towards school
- way of spending his / her time off
- relationship to parents and teachers
- opinion about politics
- view of the future

(Write about 120 words) (15)

15. Underline the four sentences with the wrong word order and correct them. (4)

a) Bob met last Saturday his girl-friend Sarah at the cinema.

b) Tony reported the police the accident.

c) Sarah explained the situation to her mother.

d) Yesterday I saw on television a film.

e) The dog brings the stick his master.

Lösungen

A Mengenbezeichnungen (Seite 6)

1. **a)** any, any, some **b)** any, some **c)** some, any **d)** any **e)** any, some **f)** some

2. **a)** Would you like some more milk? **b)** I'd like (to have) some more tea but without any sugar. **c)** Tom saw some hens on the farm, but no geese. **d)** Did you buy any books or CDs in town?

3. **a)** someone **b)** anywhere, anywhere **c)** something, anything **d)** something, anything, anything **e)** something, anything **f)** something, anything, something **g)** anyone, somewhere **h)** anyone **i)** someone

4. **a)** many, a lot of **b)** much, much **c)** many, many **d)** much, much **e)** many, many **f)** a lot of

5. **a)** a few **b)** a few **c)** a few **d)** a little **e)** a little

6. **a)** every **b)** Each **c)** each **d)** Every **e)** each **f)** each **g)** Every

7. **a)** Everyone in our family has got a car. **b)** Driving-schools can be found everywhere. **c)** It's impossible for a candidate to know everything. **d)** Today everyone must know something about cars.

8. **a)** anyone, anyone, someone, someone **b)** any, some **c)** anything, something **d)** somewhere **e)** everything **f)** everywhere

9. **a)** How much milk is there left? **b)** There is a lot of milk in the fridge, but only a little apple juice. **c)** There are only a few onions left. **d)** How many shall I buy? **e)** You must hurry because there isn't much time until the meal.

10. **a)** Michael works twenty hours in total. **b)** They are from India and English is their second language.

11. How much is the ticket?

12. **a)** How much is the new foreign language program(me)? **b)** Thank you very much.

13. **a)** Das Leben in Amerika hat sich während der letzten paar Jahrzehnte nicht verändert. **b)** Sie verdienen nicht genug Geld, um für jemanden zu bezahlen. **c)** Aber das wird nur möglich sein, wenn sie Länder wie … schlagen, von deren Spieler auch einige … spielen. **d)** Jedes Mal ist das Hauptereignis der Eröffnungsfeier … .

14. **a)** ~~Every~~ ➧ Each **b)** ~~many~~ ➧ much **e)** ~~anyone~~ ➧ someone

B Pronomen (Seite 13)

1. **b)** your, you **c)** He, his, him **d)** She, her, her **e)** It, its, it **f)** We, our, us **g)** You, your, you **h)** They, their, them
2. **a)** He, her **b)** They, us **c)** She, him **d)** He, him **e)** We, her **f)** He, it
3. **a)** Its **b)** His **c)** your **d)** their **e)** our **f)** her, Its **g)** your **h)** My
4. **a)** Her, She **b)** His, He **c)** They, Their **d)** Their, My, I, your
5. **a)** mine **b)** yours **c)** his **d)** hers **e)** ours **f)** yours **g)** theirs
6. **a)** his **b)** yours **c)** hers **d)** ours **e)** mine **f)** theirs **g)** His **h)** yours, mine
7. **a)** ourselves **b)** themselves **c)** itself **d)** yourself **e)** myself **f)** himself **g)** herself **h)** yourselves
8. **a)** Judy asks Tom where they can meet. **b)** Tom answers that he can't remember the cafe near the station. **c)** Judy says that a lot has changed in town last year. **d)** Tom asks if they should join the youth club. **e)** Judy says that not a lot happens there. **f)** Tom wonders if they'll meet many friends there.
9. **a)** themselves **b)** each other **c)** – **d)** each other **e)** – **f)** himself
10. **a)** We haven't seen each other for a long time. **b)** I can't help you and you must do your homework yourself. **c)** I apologise if I'm late. **d)** We enjoyed ourselves very much at the party. **e)** Tom and Mary met at the cinema.
11. **a)** who **b)** which **c)** which **d)** who **e)** who **f)** which **g)** which
12. **a)** who **b)** whose **c)** whose **d)** whose **e)** who **f)** whose **g)** whose
13. **a)** – **b)** – **c)** – **d)** which **e)** – **f)** who **g)** – **h)** who **i)** –
14. **a)** John visited the town he was brought up in. **b)** The girl you spoke to is from form 9C. **c)** This is the bus we came on. **d)** The country you are pointing to is Ireland. **e)** Is this the book you are interested in? **f)** The tourists Emma was talking to were from India. **g)** India is a country I don't know very much about. **h)** The keys you are looking for are on the shelf.
15. **a)** Simon, who is Emma's pen-friend, lives in New York. **b)** Jennifer, whose sister is in my class, will be 16 next week. **c)** Darren, who you met yesterday, joined our club. **d)** These bikes, which belong to my friends, are new.
16. **a)** – **b)** herself **c)** – **d)** themselves **e)** – **f)** – **g)** themselves **h)** herself **i)** themselves
17. **a)** The guests felt very hungry. **b)** Mr Brown mixed himself a cocktail. **c)** He couldn't remember having met so many nice people. **d)** He and his friend haven't seen each other for many years. **e)** When the bell rang, Mr Brown went to the door himself and opened it.

18. **a)** whose **b)** who **c)** which **d)** which **e)** whose

19. **a)** The boy, who broke his arm yesterday, must stay in hospital. **b)** The young man, who rang up last night, wanted to speak to my sister. **c)** A car hit a cat which was running across the road. **d)** In the pub there were five men who were dirty and dangerous. **e)** They were waiting with Jake whose friend was a beggar. **f)** The men saw two police cars which stopped outside. **g)** The police interviewed a man who they thought had stolen a car.

20. **a)** The book (which, that) I read is very thrilling. **b)** The story (which / that) Simon (has) told isn't true. **c)** The girl (who / that) Simon danced with comes from France. **d)** Emma, whose sister is in Scotland at the moment, is my friend. **e)** The young man, who was injured in the accident, is in hospital.

21. **a)** … is a person who runs a firm. **b)** … are people who come to another country to live there. **c)** … is a woman who works in the home. **d)** …is a huge animal which lived long ago. **e)** … is someone who breaks into houses. **f)** … is a building which is very high. **g)** … is a person who is one of the first to go to an unknown country. **h)** … is someone whose hobby is working with computers.

22. **a)** who, which **b)** which **c)** that (which) **d)** which (that)

23. **a)** The athletes, who had competed in the Games, arrived in their home town. **b)** Rachel whose team had won a medal was dancing around happily. **c)** The winner was interviewed after the competition, which had been really exciting.

24. **a)** …is a person who protects someone or something. **b)** … is something (i.e. some money) which you owe to someone. **c)** … is someone who knows all about something. **d)** … is little pieces of paper which are thrown about. **e)** … is a young person who is between 12 and 20 years. **f)** … are adverts which are broadcast on TV or radio.

25. **a)** Die Fabrik beschäftigt 13000 Leute, die billige Plastikschuhe tragen, weil keiner sich die Schuhe leisten kann, die sie herstellen. **b)** "Für euch in Europa sind die Schuhe, die wir herstellen, ein Sinnbild für Freiheit," sagt sie. **c)** Die Fans werden die Begeisterung fühlen, die diesen Sport zum schnellst wachsenden gemacht hat. **d)** Anna, die die Lehrer als äußerst gescheit beschreiben, ist vielleicht eine Ausnahme. **e)** Ihr früherer Englischlehrer sagt, dass es da Kinder gibt, die viel länger bleiben müssen.

26. **a)** ~~who~~ is standing… ➧ which is standing **b)** ~~for it I've been waiting~~ ➧ I've been waiting for **d)** ~~who I was speaking~~ ➧ who I was speaking to **f)** ~~we met at the party who is my girlfriend~~ ➧ who we met at the party, is my girlfriend.

C Adjektiv – Adverb (Seite 27)

1. **a)** the tallest, excellent, older **b)** the youngest, more difficult, stronger **c)** the prettiest, more expensive, more, as (good) as **d)** more ambitious, less, fewer **e)** the most important, better.

2. **a)** happily **b)** quietly **c)** in a friendly way **d)** fluently **e)** well **f)** carefully **g)** safely **h)** quickly.

3. **a)** easy, easily, easy **b)** angry, angrily **c)** well, good **d)** usual, usually **e)** slow, slowly.

4. **a)** Now I can understand English well. **b)** My grammar isn't perfect yet. **c)** But I can speak fluently. **d)** I must still learn to spell difficult words correctly.

5. **a)** really boring **b)** terribly strict **c)** extremely difficult **d)** awfully good, really quickly.

6. **a)** high, highly **b)** near, nearly **c)** hard, hardly **d)** late, late, lately **e)** fair, fairly.

7. **a)** more carefully **b)** faster **c)** better **d)** more quickly **e)** harder **f)** earlier **g)** more seriously.

8. **a)** (the) fastest **b)** (the) most **c)** (the) farthest **d)** (the) most beautifully **e)** (the) most sensibly **f)** (the) best.

9. **a)** happy **b)** sad **c)** wonderful **d)** delicious **e)** good, loud **f)** happily **g)** carefully **h)** nice.

10. **a)** (Munich is) bigger than Edinburgh. **b)** It is the biggest city in Bavaria. **c)** There is one of the most important museums in Germany. **d)** Maybe they will build a completely new football stadium.

11. **a)** Ich hatte nicht die geringste Vorstellung, wie die Indianer leben, bevor ich das Reservat besuchte. **b)** Die Navajos sind einer der berühmtesten Indianerstämme. **c)** Immer mehr von ihnen wollen in Reservaten leben. **d)** Es ist furchtbar, wenn man hört, dass Indianer die höchste Alkoholrate im Land haben. **e)** Sie haben ein niedrigeres Bildungsniveau als weiße Amerikaner und schlechtere Gesundheitsbedingungen.

12. **a)** regularly **b)** popular, extremely warm **c)** good, really, excellent.

13. **a)** better, (the) quickest **b)** more quickly, more accurately **c)** worst, laziest, cleverer **d)** most, best, hard, effectively.

14. **a)** badly hurt **b)** particularly **c)** immediately

15. **a)** confident **b)** tragical **c)** foolish **d)** safest **e)** dangerous.

16. **a)** most important **b)** farther **c)** most popular **d)** hottest.

17. **a)** than **b)** worst **c)** really remarkable **d)** national **e)** more **f)** deep

18. huge animal. (It was) at least six metres tall and thirty metres long. (It had) thick legs like an elephant (and a) tiny head.

19. **a)** Als Spielberg zum ersten Mal daran dachte seinen wichtigsten Film, "Schindlers Liste", zu drehen, war er nicht sicher, ob er es schaffen / machen könnte. **b)** Da er glaubte, dass andere Kollegen für ein so ernstes Thema besser qualifiziert / geeignet wären, versuchte er die Rechte an erfahrenere Regisseure zu verkaufen. **c)** Keiner von ihnen war jedoch wirklich interessiert. **d)** Viele seiner Freunde sagten ihm, er würde bestimmt scheitern. **e)** Aber je mehr Zweifel sie äußerten, desto sicherer wurde Spielberg.

20. **a)** ~~beautifuller~~ ➧ more beautiful **b)** ~~good~~ ➧ well **c)** ~~well~~ ➧ good **d)** richtig **e)** ~~as~~ ➧ than **f)** richtig.

D Zeitformen (Seite 38)

1. **a)** plays **b)** goes **c)** sits **d)** don't watch **e)** visit **f)** don't stay

2. **a)** I usually get up at seven o'clock. **b)** My school bus goes at twenty to eight. **c)** The first lesson always begins at eight o'clock. **d)** In the afternoon, I go to football training. **e)** After supper, I watch a little TV. **f)** On Saturday I don't get up so early as / because we don't go to school.

3. **a)** is tidying, is raining **b)** is lying (lie ➧ lying!), is reading **c)** are working, are repairing **d)** is playing, are listening **e)** are you doing, am repeating.

4. **a)** I'm just making a cake. **b)** Mother is celebrating her birthday. **c)** Susan is doing some shopping. **d)** She is buying coffee and flowers. **e)** Only Paul isn't doing anything. – Oh yes, he's playing table tennis.

5. **a)** decided **b)** didn't walk, went **c)** were not, was **d)** met, sat **e)** told, didn't understand, was **f)** entered, danced, stayed.

6. **a)** Last week we were in London. **b)** We visited Rock Circus and the Dungeon of London. **c)** We met some nice people and then we went to a pub. **d)** We had some sandwiches, but we didn't get any beer. **e)** The landlord wanted to see our identity cards. **f)** Then he said: "You're too young for alcohol."

7. **a)** was playing **b)** were swimming **c)** was reading **d)** was knitting **e)** was repairing **f)** were preparing.

8. **a)** was raining, went **b)** was writing, came, asked **c)** was ringing / rang, packed, ran **d)** was reading, came, looked **e)** was mending, rang.

9. **a)** have not seen **b)** has known **c)** have repaired **d)** has not tidied **e)** have been **f)** has not eaten

10. **a)** Julie is sad; she has lost her keys. **b)** We must wait; the train has not arrived yet. **c)** Is Patrick in? – He has just come home. **d)** I have tidied my room; now I can go out to play. **e)** I have had my bike for four years; it is still going well. **f)** Jenny has never been to London. What a pity!

11. **a)** have been working **b)** has been waiting **c)** has been raining **d)** have been living **e)** has been painting **f)** have been trying **g)** has been playing.

12. **a)** How long have you been learning English? – I have been learning it for five years. **b)** This book is not new. How long have you been using it? – We have been using it since the beginning of the school year. **c)** Your little brother is so dirty. – He has been playing football all morning. **d)** Your father is very tired. – He has been working in the garden all day.

13. **a)** went, had watched **b)** drove, had finished **c)** bought, had wanted **d)** phoned, had gone **e)** began, had left **f)** didn't come, had missed.

14. **a)** I am sure we will enjoy our winter holidays. **b)** I hope there will be enough snow. **c)** It will not (won't) be easy to find cheap accommodation. **d)** We will have to book the rooms next week. **e)** I will be fifteen in January. **f)** I think we will have a wonderful party in the snow.

15. **a)** Tomorrow morning there will be clouds in the mountains, **b)** but in the afternoon it will be sunny. **c)** The day after tomorrow it will be warmer, but a bit windy. **d)** There will be little change in the next few days. **e)** They are sure it won't rain.

16. **a)** Mr Miller is going to paint his house. **b)** His wife is going to buy new curtains. **c)** The children are going to attend a language course. **d)** They are not going to watch TV next Saturday. **e)** They are going to have a big party on Saturday night. **f)** They are going to have lots of food and drinks.

17. **a)** (They) are going to buy some CDs. **b)** (Helen) and her mother are going to do some shopping. Helen needs a coat. **c)** (Barbara) and her sister are going to buy tickets for the musical. They want to see the performance on Saturday.

18. **a)** met, have been going **b)** has had **c)** is working **d)** spends **e)** is saved **f)** will help.

19. did (you) arrive, came, was, are, had been living, lost, found, do (you) like, have not seen, have spent, do (you) like, do, are, helps, used, do (you) practise, am, have been playing, will join, Have, You're welcome.

20. **a)** Hello, Steven. What are you going to do in your summer holidays? **b)** I was in Canada last year and I liked the journey very much. I would like to go to Canada again. **c)** I haven't been to Canada yet. I hope I'll be able to visit my aunt in Toronto in two years.

21. **a)** held **b)** took place / had taken place **c)** have competed **d)** watch

22. **a)** lives **b)** has just come **c)** is wearing **d)** did you buy **e)** were invented **f)** had experimented **g)** having injured / injuring **h)** succeeded in getting **i)** have become.

23. **a)** She last saw him 88 years ago. **b)** He was standing on the deck of the Titanic. **c)** He hoped to see them in New York. **d)** They talk about it because it is a story of superlatives.

24. I will get a job which (that) I really enjoy. I also hope I will find a partner who (that) understands my problems and that I'll get on well with my family.

25. **a)** am writing **b)** have won **c)** would like **d)** is **e)** are **f)** is **g)** can take **h)** will come **i)** am looking forward **j)** to seeing

26. **a)** Nach vier Jahren unfreiwilliger Abwesenheit wurde Vingo S. von seiner Frau und seinen drei Kindern spektakulär daheim begrüßt. **b)** Es war das glückliche Ende einer Geschichte, die vor vier Jahre eine tragische Wendung genommen hatte, als Vingo eingesperrt wurde. **c)** Was war das Verbrechen, das er begangen hatte? **d)** Er arbeitete in der Bank seines Onkels und als sein Onkel plötzlich verschwand, wurde er angeklagt, ein Verbrecher zu sein.

27. **a)** ~~has visited~~ ➧ visited **b)** richtig **c)** ~~is~~ ➧ has been **d)** richtig **e)** ~~has~~ ➧ had **f)** ~~slept~~ ➧ was sleeping **g)** ~~listens~~ ➧ is listening.

E Fragesätze (Seite 55)

1. **a)** Does school begin at eight o'clock? **b)** Are there lessons every afternoon? **c)** Do you have lunch at school? **d)** Do you go to school on Saturday? **e)** Have you visited your twin town in Germany yet?

2. **a)** Are you interested in sports? **b)** Do you like tennis? **c)** Did you see the match last night? **d)** Do you want to play a game against me? **e)** Can you meet me at ten o'clock tomorrow?

3. **a)** When does the first lesson begin? **b)** Where can the pupils buy refreshments? **c)** Why did Andy go to the club last week? **d)** How do most pupils work? **e)** How many hours does homework take a day? **f)** How much is the school uniform / How much does the school uniform cost? **g)** How did Jennifer come to school? **h)** When must Darren get up every morning?

4. **a)** What did Simon write? **b)** What does Fred like? **c)** What did Jane buy? **d)** Who will Julia and Emma visit? **e)** What have they read? **f)** Who does Oliver help in the afternoon? **g)** What did Darren lose?

5. **a)** Who loves Julia? **b)** Who went to Italy in her summer holidays? **c)** What happened in front of the school? **d)** What begins at nine o'clock? **e)** Whose friend plays the guitar? **f)** Which bus goes to the railway station? **g)** How many children came to the birthday party?

6. **a)** Who doesn't play cricket? **b)** Which of you doesn't know the answer? **c)** Why didn't Jack stay in Dublin? **d)** When can't Sheila go home? **e)** Which books don't belong to you? **f)** How many of you don't like rugby? **g)** Who didn't come to the barbecue?

7. **a)** Where does Geoff come from? **b)** What is he good at? **c)** What / What sort of school does he go to? **d)** Who does the old Rover belong to? **e)** Who did he buy it from? **f)** What does he sometimes listen to? **g)** What are Geoff and his friends talking about? **h)** What are they afraid of?

8. **a)** isn't she **b)** hasn't she **c)** can't she **d)** is he **e)** don't they **f)** does she **g)** didn't he **h)** won't he.

9. **a)** What time do you get up every morning? **b)** How do you get to school? **c)** Do you like school? **d)** What do you do in your spare time? **e)** Which is your favourite soccer team? **f)** Do you know a German football club? **g)** Where did you learn German? **h)** Which places have you seen so far?

10. **a)** Where do you come from? **b)** Do you have brothers or sisters? **c)** How do you like Germany? **d)** What don't you like in a German school? **e)** Have you been to Europe before? **f)** What are your hobbies? **g)** How long are you staying / going to stay? **h)** Have you got a boyfriend?

11. **a)** Do you know any foreign languages? **b)** What schools did you go to? **c)** Which were your favourite subjects at school? **d)** Which subjects didn't you like at all? **e)** Where do you usually spend your weekends? **f)** Why would you like to become a secretary? **g)** How are you going to come to the office every day? **h)** When will you be able to start work?

12. **a)** How much is the ticket? **b)** Where can I buy it? **c)** When can I use it? **d)** Have you ever used the Travelcard yourself?

13. **a)** When did you win your first medal? **b)** Do you know any sportsmen who take drugs? **c)** Why did you decide to become an athlete? **d)** How long do you practise every day?

14. **a)** Where are the nearest motels? **b)** How many visitors were there at the Route 66 festival last month? **c)** Were there any serious accidents nearby? **d)** Have you seen the TV series ROUTE 66?

15. **a)** Can I help you? **b)** Are there any special offers? **c)** How much is the new foreign language programme? **d)** Can you recommend it? **e)** Which exercises do customers in the U.S.A. prefer?

16. **a)** Why have you taken up a job? **b)** Are there sometimes shoplifters in your store? **c)** What is your job like, in general?

17. **a)** ~~Who~~ ➧ Where **b)** richtig **c)** do ➧ (What) do you do **d)** richtig **e)** like ➧ do you like.

F Modalverben (Seite 66)

1. **a)** can, can't **b)** will be able to **c)** wasn't able to / couldn't **d)** can, can't / aren't able to **e)** weren't able to / couldn't.

2. **a)** I'm sorry I can't help you. **b)** Yesterday I couldn't play tennis because it was raining. **c)** I haven't been able to phone Tom yet; I can't find his telephone number. **d)** Next Saturday I won't be able to come to training. **e)** I could help you if you rang me beforehand.

3. **a)** Can, mustn't / can't **b)** mustn't **c)** can, aren't allowed to **d)** may, can **e)** were allowed to **f)** will be allowed to **g)** haven't been allowed to.

4. **a)** During the week I am not allowed to go out / mustn't go out in the evening. **b)** At the weekend I can stay out / I am allowed to stay out until ten o'clock. **c)** Last Friday I was allowed to go to the concert. **d)** Next year I will be allowed to go to Italy with my girlfriends.

5. **a)** must / have to / are having to **b)** had to, Did … have to, didn't **c)** had to, didn't have to **d)** has had to **e)** will have to.

6. **a)** We must / have to learn a lot this month. **b)** Yesterday we had to write a long essay. **c)** Tomorrow we will have to do a difficult maths exercise. **d)** We have had to prepare a project for two weeks. **e)** On Friday, we need not come / don't have to come to school.

7. **a)** may **b)** may have **c)** might **d)** might have **e)** may **f)** might have.

8. **a)** should **b)** should not **c)** should **d)** should have **e)** should not have **f)** should have.

9. **a)** can, needn't, can **b)** needn't, can **c)** needn't, can **d)** mustn't **e)** Can, mustn't **f)** must, mustn't.

10. **a)** shouldn't **b)** should have **c)** needn't **d)** mustn't, should **e)** mustn't, should **f)** must, mustn't.

11. **a)** Dürfen wir hier sitzen? – Oh ja. **b)** Vielleicht regnet es morgen. Sollen wir unsere Pläne ändern? **c)** Könntest du mir bitte die Bushaltestelle zeigen? **d)** Jennifer konnte nicht zu unserer Party kommen, weil sie letzte Woche krank war. **e)** Du darfst die Tür nicht offen lassen, Barbara. Es ist windig. **f)** Du brauchst mir nicht zu helfen, Darren. Ich kann es selber machen.

12. **a)** Ich kann meinen Schlüssel nicht finden. Ich muss ihn vergessen haben. **b)** Es ist schade, dass du die Vase fallen gelassen hast. Du hättest vorsichtiger sein sollen. **c)** Du hättet nicht so früh kommen müssen. Das Treffen beginnt in einer halben Stunde. **d)** Ich winkte Peter auf der Straße zu, aber er reagierte nicht; vielleicht war er in Eile. **e)** Der Unfall war furchtbar. Er hätte noch schlimmer sein können, wenn der Krankenwagen nicht (so) schnell gekommen wäre. **f)** Sheila kann die Verabredung / das Datum nicht vergessen haben; sie ist so zuverlässig.

13. a) I can switch off the lights when I leave the room to save electricity. b) Everyone will have his spacecraft in the garage. There will be pills for all kinds of illnesses. c) We have to close the windows in our classroom, switch on the lights and leave the room at once.

14. a) should, can b) must not, could c) should.

15. a) Liebe Mutti, vielleicht erinnerst du dich daran, dass Jack vor drei Monaten beschloss, einen Computer zu kaufen. b) Seither hat es einen radikalen Wandel in seiner Haltung gegenüber seiner Familie gegeben. c) Jeden Tag verbringt er Stunden über Stunden an seinem Computer und probiert neue Programme aus. d) Sogar an den Wochenenden kann Jack nicht widerstehen, vor seinem Bildschirm zu sitzten. e) Ich denke, es wäre eine gute Idee, Onkel Herbert um Rat zu fragen. f) Er sollte in der Lage sein, mir zu sagen, was ich tun soll.

16. a) musst nicht ➧ darfst nicht b) darf ➧ vielleicht (schneit es) c) richtig d) Konntest ➧ Könntest e) soll ➧ sollte.

G Passiv (Seite 76)

1. a) is being cut b) are cut c) are repaired d) is being repaired e) is being tested f) are not tested

2. a) was being cleaned b) was cleaned c) was being built d) were built e) are served f) were being served

3. a) have been stolen b) has been written c) have been given d) have been solved e) has been done f) has not been allowed g) has not been found h) has never been invited

4. a) won't / will not be repaired b) will be shown c) will be asked d) will be smashed e) will be opened f) will be invited g) will not / won't be completed h) will be developed

5. a) should be washed b) cannot be shut c) ought to be tidied d) could not be seen e) must be looked after f) might be invited g) has to be pulled down h) cannot be learned i) ought not to be laughed at j) can only be done k) must be sold l) has to be done m) must not be entered n) could not be put out

6. a) is understood b) will be invited c) was shown d) is earned e) will be won f) was built g) has not been finished h) will be finished i) must be discussed j) is not taught k) has always been l) has been made m) is being repaired n) was being built

7. a) took place b) were celebrated c) took place d) were, were held e) included f) were treated g) renewed h) have been held i) applies, must be built j) have been invited k) are shown

8. **a)** Man bot Frau Carter eine bessere Arbeit an. **b)** Gestern Abend wurde der Doktor geholt. **c)** Man wird der Mannschaft eine große Möglichkeit bieten. **d)** Mr Johnson soll (angeblich) nächste Woche nach Paris fliegen. **e)** Man sagte, dass Herr Brown einen anderen Job finden würde.

9. **a)** A ferry to England must be booked very early. **b)** A letter was written to me. **c)** I was offered a good hotel. **d)** I will be sent a good offer soon. **e)** My friend has also been invited.

10. **a)** was fascinated **b)** was asked **c)** were damaged (had been damaged) **d)** was interviewed **e)** were taken **f)** was chosen (had been chosen)

11. **a)** Man wird dir wahrscheinlich später glauben. **b)** Ich habe einen Film gemacht, der der teuerste genannt worden ist. **c)** Die meisten Stuntleute wurden ernstlich verletzt. **d)** Seit damals werden die Olympischen Spiele wieder abgehalten. **e)** Man bezahlt Eni 25 Cents die Stunde. **f)** Sie werden oft gezwungen, bis Mitternacht zu arbeiten. (Sie müssen…) **g)** Zwei Finger sind abgetrennt worden.

12. **a)** ~~is worn~~ ➧ are worn **b)** ~~is being frying~~ ➧ is being fried **d)** ~~are drove~~ ➧ are driven **e)** ~~must be keeping~~ ➧ must be kept **f)** Tony sagte, er sei ein guter Spieler. ➧ Man sagt, Tony sei ein guter Spieler. (Tony soll ein guter Spieler sein.)

H Gerund – Infinitiv (Seite 85)

1. **a)** smoking, smoking **b)** reading, reading **c)** getting, getting **d)** playing, cycling.

2. **a)** Playing tennis is Rebecca's favourite sport. **b)** She doesn't mind playing in the rain. **c)** Simon likes reading adventure stories. **d)** But his hobby is playing the guitar. **e)** Peter often comes to school late. He hates getting up early.

3. **a)** for coming **b)** of travelling **c)** on paying **d)** to working **e)** for driving **f)** in winning **g)** of going **h)** to writing.

4. **a)** of being **b)** of losing **c)** of playing **d)** at swimming **e)** to working **f)** in earning **g)** of learning **h)** about dancing.

5. **a)** catching **b)** of winning **c)** (in) selling **d)** for finishing **e)** for being **f)** of using **g)** of pushing **h)** in visiting.

6. **a)** Du kannst dein Englisch verbessern, indem du effektiver lernst. **b)** Du kannst kein guter Fußballer werden, ohne viel zu trainieren. **c)** Die Buben waren verärgert, nachdem sie das Spiel verloren hatten. **d)** Du solltest dich konzentrieren, anstatt die ganze Zeit zu schwätzen. **e)** Sie reinigten ihre Tische, bevor sie das Zimmer verließen. **f)** Sie fingen an zu lachen, als sie die Neuigkeit hörten.

7. **a)** play **b)** to join **c)** enter **d)** to enter **e)** to do, start **f)** go, to stay **g)** to take, return **h)** to have, show.

8. **a)** The girls decided to meet next Saturday. **b)** Helen would like to visit her German pen-friend. **c)** We had to walk home yesterday. **d)** We needn't go to school on Saturday. **e)** Peter is ill; he had better call his doctor. **f)** Ellen used to live with her parents; today she has a flat of her own.

9. **a)** her to get up **b)** me to use **c)** her to be **d)** me to give **e)** them to be **f)** him to be **g)** them to have.

10. **a)** Darren asked his sister to be quiet. **b)** He expected her not to disturb him with his homework. **c)** Later he said: "I want you to help me". **d)** She asked: "Would you like me to copy the text?" **e)** She advised him to repeat the vocabulary. **f)** Then she asked: "Do you want us to read the text together?"

11. **a)** for children / them to smoke **b)** for you to go home **c)** for him to come **d)** for Susan / her to carry **e)** important for Patrick / him to learn.

12. **a)** Es ist wichtig für junge Menschen, Fremdsprachen zu lernen. **b)** Das Wetter war zu schlecht, als dass das Flugzeug abheben / starten konnte. **c)** Warte(t) bitte nicht darauf, dass ich zum Essen zurück bin. **d)** Es war keine Zeit, dass wir uns den Film ansahen. Wir mussten fort. **e)** Geht es in Ordnung, wenn ich bleibe?

13. **a)** how to get **b)** what to do **c)** where to put **d)** to arrive, to leave **e)** to sing.

14. **a)** James wusste nicht, welchen Weg er einschlagen sollte. Er hatte seine Landkarte verloren. **b)** Er bat einen Polizisten um Hilfe. Das war das Beste, was er tun konnte. **c)** Der Polizist sagte ihm, wo er gehen sollte. **d)** Helen hatte keine Idee, wie sie sich auf das Interview / Vorstellungsgespräch vorbereiten sollte. **e)** Sie hatte auch vergessen, wo sie hingehen sollte.

15. **a)** flying, travelling, to see **b)** going, flying, to visit, to be **c)** going, to stay, to build, doing **d)** smoking, to smoke, ruining, to be / I'll be **e)** to sitting, for going, asking **f)** to learn, to visit, to talking.

16. **a)** Do you like playing tennis / Are you fond of playing tennis? **b)** Do you also dislike / hate going to the disco? **c)** Are you interested in taking part in a summer camp? **d)** Are you good at swimming? **e)** Do you want to participate in the championships? **f)** Are you looking forward to seeing me soon?

17. **a)** (I) would like to obtain / get further information. **b)** (I) want to book a holiday apartment. **c)** (My) parents would like to find out the price for four persons. **d)** (I) look forward to receiving / getting an answer soon.

18. My home town is (not) situated in a very beautiful area. There is (not) a lot to do. The people are (not) very friendly.

19. **a)** Darren kann das Rauchen nicht aufgeben. **b)** Julie ist daran interessiert, nette Leute zu treffen. **c)** Petra bestand die Prüfung, indem sie tüchtig lernte. **d)** Es lohnt sich nicht, diese Platten zu kaufen. **e)** Wie wär's mit etwas Kaffee / , wenn wir Kaffee trinken? **f)** Es hat keinen Zweck, länger zu warten. **g)** Großvater hat früher in einem alten Landhaus gewohnt. **h)** Craig wird wahrscheinlich gewinnen / der Sieger sein. **i)** Stuart spielt gern Keyboard. **j)** Jonathan steht ungern / nicht gern früh auf.

20. **a)** My father used to smoke as a young man. **b)** I am used to getting up early. **c)** You can use this tool for cutting. d) It's no use waiting for Susan any longer.

21. **a)** to influence **b)** to stop **c)** reading / he had read **d)** to talk **e)** listening / in listening **f)** to support

22. My favourite hobbies are soccer and tennis. I'm fond of soccer because I like playing in a team. Playing tennis is good exercise for me, and I can meet lots of people in our local club.

23. **a)** I agree because you can buy things that are your taste, or you can travel where you like without your parents. / I disagree because my parents are willing to give me enough pocket money and I want to concentrate on my school work. **b)** I agree because you have to work hard at school to get reasonable marks. / I can't agree because this is a question of organising ability to do well in both.

24. **a)** Zwei der großen Rätsel über die Jahrhunderte waren, wie man den Weg über die Meere findet und wie man die genaue Uhrzeit bestimmen kann. **b)** Nachdem er 43 Jahre in seinem Observatorium gearbeitet hatte, legte der königliche Astronom John Flamsteed 1676 den Meridian von Greenwich fest. **c)** Dies versetzte jeden Kapitän in die Lage, die genaue Position seines Schiffes zu kennen. **d)** 1884 wurde beschlossen, alle Uhren nach der Zeit von Greenwich zu stellen.

25. **a)** to play ➧ playing **b)** to get ➧ to getting **c)** richtig **d)** that his friends help ➧ his friends to help **e)** to see ➧ to seeing.

I If-Sätze (Seite 100)

1. **a)** will understand **b)** works **c)** don't try **d)** will you do **e)** will be angry

2. **a)** If the weather is good, I'll stay at the seaside. **b)** If we go by car, we'll certainly visit the Lake District. **c)** If we find a nice place, we'll go camping. **d)** We will need a bigger tent if my friends come with me. **e)** If there is a chance, we'll take a boat trip on the canal. **f)** We'll have a look around if we pass a pretty village. **g)** If we have time, we'll go to lovely pubs in the evenings. **h)** We'll put on waterproof clothing if it rains. **i)** If I take photos, I'll send you some.

3. **a)** If I pass my exam, I'll go on holiday. **b)** If I have a lot of time, I'll sleep longer in the morning. **c)** If my friends give a big party, I'll try to get invited. **d)** If I visit the USA, I'll go to New York and the Rocky Mountains. **e)** If I'm at home, I'll phone you at 7 o'clock.

4. **a)** had **b)** would not ask **c)** didn't train **e)** could your friend do **f)** were

5. **a)** If I won a lot of money on the lottery, I would travel round the world. **b)** If I travelled round the world, I would see a lot of interesting countries. **c)** If I had a chance, I would first fly to New York. **d)** If I were (was) in New York, I would try to get tickets for the Metropolitan Opera. **e)** If I went to the Metropolitan Opera, I would meet many nice people. **f)** If I talked to many Americans, I would improve my knowledge of English.

6. **a)** If I had a lot of money, I would travel to New York. **b)** If I was in New York, I would take a lot of photographs. **c)** If I was in Manhattan, I could see many skyscrapers.

7. **a)** would have told **b)** had not come **c)** could have come **d)** would not have been **e)** had not worked

8. **a)** If I had saved more money, I would have spent more time in Ireland. **b)** I would have got better information if I had read books about that country. **c)** If I had had better information, I would have visited more interesting places. **d)** If I had had the chance, I would have taken my car with me. **e)** If I had taken my car with me, I would have seen more of the countryside. **f)** If the weather hadn't been so bad, I would have gone to one of the islands. **g)** If I had found one of the "singing pubs", I would have spent an evening there.

9. **a)** If I had had more time in my holidays, I would have travelled to Ireland. **b)** Craig could have met Rosie in the cafe if he had been in town. **c)** If they had met, they would have gone to the cinema.

10. travel; will visit, will take, go; had; would fly, was (were), would stay; had been; would have tried, would have gone, had invited

11. will travel; cannot say; will come; will only give, pass; learnt, was (were), would pay, did not spend; would be glad, didn't remind

12. **a)** What would you do Rosie if you had enough money? **b)** If I had as much money as you, I would go on holiday twice a year. **c)** We can travel together if you take your holiday in July. **d)** If we travel through England, we will visit our friends in Durham. **e)** If we had the chance, we could take our bikes with us.

13. **a)** would attend **b)** will disturb **c)** wasn't

14. **a)** would have reacted **b)** was (were) **c)** tried **d)** had started, would have covered **e)** had been, would have escaped

15. **a)** I would stay there because I wouldn't like to leave my friends. **b)** If I were in London, I would go by bus because I could see more of the town. **c)** I don't think I would go because I'm not good at English. My parents would not let me go because they don't have the money and they are afraid of the high crime rate.

16. **a)** If I won first prize in a competition, I would definitely go on holiday but I would also save some of the money. **b)** If a cyclist knocked me over, I would probably shout at him and then I would try to walk home. **c)** If the police stopped me, I would tell them that my friend had been wearing a helmet when we left but it had fallen off. We were driving back to find it. **d)** If I saw a lost child at a fair, I would try to make sure he (she) was safe by taking him (her) to a policeman.

17. **a)** would ask ➧ asked **b)** don't speak ➧ won't speak **c)** have been ➧ had been **d)** travel ➧ will travel

J Indirekte Rede (Seite 111)

1. **a)** Mrs Nolan says (that) she wants a bigger house. **b)** Sam adds (that) he needs a room of his own. **c)** The children ask where they are moving to. **d)** Mr Nolan remarks (that) he guesses they will have to look for a larger place. **e)** Mrs Nolan has always said (that) they must have a house with six rooms. **f)** Judy says (that) she is old enough to have a room of her own. **g)** Mrs Nolan wants to know if they are going to buy a new house.

2. **a)** Mr Nolan asked if they wanted a bigger house. **b)** Mrs Nolan answered (that) it was absolutely necessary for them to have six rooms. **c)** Sam added (that) he saw (had seen) an advertisement in the newspaper. **d)** Judy had said (that) she had always wanted a room of her own. **e)** She declared (that) she liked to have a room with a large window. **f)** Sam wanted to know when they bought a new house. **g)** Mrs Nolan remarked (that) she thought the estate agent had got many houses for sale.

3. **a)** Mr Nolan said (that) they would buy a new house if the bank gave them the money. **b)** Judy asked what they would do with the old one. **c)** Her father replied (that) he would go to the estate agent's and try to sell it. **d)** Mrs Nolan remarked (that) they had to get a good price for the old house. **e)** Her husband said (that) she didn't have to worry and he could easily find a buyer. **f)** Sam asked if he might have a room upstairs. **g)** His father answered that he had to wait until they had got an offer. **h)** Mrs Nolan added that if it was possible, each of them would get his own room.

4. **a)** Mrs Nolan said she didn't like that place any more. **b)** She added they were (had been) reading all those advertisements. **c)** Her husband mentioned he didn't like it there either. **d)** Then he added he would have a look at the newspaper that day. **e)** Sam said his friends showed (had shown) him his room the day before. **f)** Grandma declared she would move out the following day. **g)** Father replied they would have a larger house the following week. **h)** Grandmother said he just said (had said) the same the previous month. **i)** Mrs Nolan said they missed (had missed) a good chance the year before.

5. **a)** Mrs Nolan told Sam to listen to her. **b)** Judy asked Sam to leave her alone. **c)** Sam told her not to lose her temper. **d)** Judy told him not to make such a fuss about everything. **e)** Mrs Nolan asked Judy to speak about that problem with her father. **f)** Father told them to stop quarrelling. **g)** Mrs Nolan told Sam to go upstairs when he had finished. **h)** She told Judy to switch off the lights before she went to bed.

6. **a)** … if he knew that Mum was looking for a new house. **b)** Sam answered (that) he (had) heard her talking about that matter the day before. **c)** Judy asked if Sam wanted to move. **d)** Sam answered (that) he didn't want to leave there. **e)** Judy wanted to know if he knew how much a new house would cost. **f)** Sam answered that he didn't, but he didn't think they could afford to buy a new one. **g)** Judy said that if they voted against that plan, Mum and Dad couldn't refuse their proposals. **h)** Sam asked what she was going to propose. **i)** Judy replied (that) they could convert the attic into a big room. **j)** Sam exclaimed (that) that was wonderful and he would tell Steve immediately.

7. … he had spoken to you about an offer the week before. He said you had asked him if he could find a suitable house for you. He added (that) he had got a wonderful place which he was sure would be large enough for our family. Then he asked if I could talk about it with my family. Then he asked me to let him know when we had made up our mind to move into that lovely home.

8. **a)** I'd like to buy a new house. **b)** We would be very happy if we had our own room. **c)** Could I have a room on the first floor (upstairs)? **d)** It depends on how many rooms we will have. **e)** How much will a new house cost? **f)** We'll have to save a lot of money, but I think we'll have managed it by next year. **g)** Everyone of us should help.

9. Mr Schmid would like to visit Yosemite National Park tomorrow and he would like to know the best way to get there. – Es ist natürlich kein Problem, mit dem Auto dorthin zu gelangen, aber die Touristen bevorzugen gewöhnlich einen unserer Busausflüge. – Okay then, he will go by bus. Is he allowed to take photos? – An den interessantesten Plätzen gibt es einen Aufenthalt. Ihr Reiseleiter wird ihnen genug Zeit geben, herumzuspazieren und die Landschaft zu genießen. – Mr Schmid thanks a lot for your help and says good-bye.

10. **a)** I am going ➧ I was going **b)** where had his wife gone ➧ where his wife had gone **c)** Mrs Baker ~~says~~ Tom ➧ Mrs Baker tells Tom **d)** told the boys ~~to don't~~ talk so loud ➧ told the boys not to talk so loud. **f)** next year ➧ the following year.

K Partizipialsätze (Seite 121)

1. **a)** The train leaving … **b)** The man knocking … **c)** The street leading … **d)** In our town there is a lot of pollution caused … **e)** Do you know the girl talking … **f)** Films made in Hollywood …
2. **a)** Being tired **b)** Feeling frightened **c)** Wanting to catch **d)** having lost his wallet **e)** Not knowing the way **f)** Being injured.
3. **a)** While walking … **b)** Before handing in … **c)** (On) hearing the telephone Lucy stopped working … **d)** After having helped / After helping / Having helped his mother, Andrew cycled … **e)** (when) crossing … **f)** Seeing the taxi Mr Winter stopped …
4. **a)** Sheila walked down the lane singing. **b)** Darren and Helen were in the kitchen washing the dishes. **c)** Mr Miller sat in his armchair smoking his pipe. **d)** Craig went to bed hoping to fall asleep immediately. **e)** Karen picked up the telephone looking forward to hearing her mother's voice.
5. **a)** living **b)** Feeling **c)** sold **d)** spoken **e)** travelling **f)** injured.
6. **a)** People who drive to work … **b)** The girl who is sitting … **c)** The car which was stopped … **d)** Trains which go to Glasgow … **e)** The flag which is flying … **f)** Books which are bought …
7. **a)** As / Because we wanted to get home … **b)** As / Because he didn't know … **c)** When he saw the old man … **d)** While they were listening to Helen's story … **e)** When he came into the room … **f)** While we were sitting in the pub …
8. **a)** Da / Weil sie müde war, setzte sich Helen eine Zeitlang hin. **b)** Peter saß auf seiner Couch und las ein Buch. **c)** Matthew ging die Straße entlang und pfiff. **d)** Da / weil sie selber einsam war, verstand Jane Helens Problem. **e)** Leute, die das Museum besuchen wollen, müssen die Türglocke läuten. **f)** Da / Weil er überzeugt war, Recht zu haben, gab George nicht nach. **g)** Da / weil er sich sehr müde fühlte, ging Geoff sofort ins Bett. **h)** Da / Weil sie das Fußballspiel nicht verlieren wollten, trainierten Patrick und seine Freunde letzte Woche dreimal. **i)** Ein Auto, das vor zehn Jahren gekauft wurde, ist heute nicht viel wert. **j)** Da / Weil der Tag schön war, beschlossen die Kinder im Garten zu spielen.
9. **a)** called **b)** Thinking **c)** leaving **d)** rushing **e)** putting **f)** Resisting **g)** snapping **h)** realising.

10. **a)** Feeling stronger and more energetic these days senior citizens don't want to give up their jobs. **b)** (As they are) Working for money a lot of American teenagers are less dependent on their parents.

11. **a)** Die 15-jährige Eni bemalt die Sohlen von Sportschuhen, wobei sie in der schrecklichen Hitze schwitzt. **b)** Die Fabrik beschäftigt 13.000 Menschen, die Plastikschuhe tragen, weil sich keiner von ihnen die Schuhe, die sie herstellen, leisten kann. **c)** Man bezahlt Eni 25 Cents pro Stunde. Im Vergleich dazu / Verglichen damit kostet ein Paar Tennisschuhe ungefähr 150 Dollar. **d)** Es gibt viele Unfälle, die durch alte Maschinen verursacht werden.

12. **a)** which ➧ (the film) made / the film which was made **b)** richtig **c)** As ➧ Being cold **d)** breaking ➧ broken.

L Wortstellung (Seite 129)

1. **a)** Ian plays the guitar. **b)** Jane is doing her homework. **c)** Ian can speak Russian. **d)** Mary has got a dog and a cat.

2. **a)** The boys seldom go swimming. **b)** Susan never drank coffee. **c)** Susan and Jill always do their homework together. **d)** Mr Miller can usually finish the crossword puzzle.

3. **a)** Mr Talbot often works in the garden at the weekend. **b)** Tom never eats cornflakes in the morning. **c)** Jean usually likes to listen to music in her room in the evening. **d)** Mr Brown always reads his newspaper after breakfast on Sunday. **e)** Mr Brown sometimes makes tea in the kitchen on Sunday morning.

4. **a)** My brother always goes to school by bus. **b)** I never have school on Saturday. **c)** I sometimes make tea in the kitchen on Sunday. **d)** My friend often plays football in the stadium in the afternoon. **e)** We seldom go swimming in the river in summer. **f)** Our family usually goes cycling together in our holidays.

5. **a)** The incident happened on a platform in London last night. **b)** A crowd of young people were behaving very rudely. **c)** An old lady slowly went up to the loudest youth. **d)** She found his behaviour terribly bad. **e)** The other travellers quietly read their papers. **f)** They simply concentrated on their papers. **g)** It was really surprising that they said nothing. **h)** The old lady's reaction was absolutely right. **i)** The stationmaster could have told the youths to behave more politely.

6. **a)** Tom showed the controller his ticket. **b)** Jane gave her mother some beautiful flowers for her birthday. **c)** Mr Molyneux teaches the pupils French. **d)** Mr Moneymaker promises his workers higher wages. **e)** Sam sent a letter to Mary, not to Jane. **f)** Tony lends £10 to his friend,

not to his brother. **g)** Mr Brown will sell his uncle his old car. **h)** Mother tells her children a nice story.

7. **a)** … the accident to the policeman. **b)** … the problem to her father. **c)** … tea to milk. **d)** … himself to the landlady. **e)** … another detail to the report. **f)** … good morning to the teacher.

8. **a)** Hundreds of fans had come to the airport before the plane landed. **b)** The fans got extremely excited when the singers came in sight. **c)** The singers wanted to go to their hotel but they had to sing a song first. **d)** The guitarist didn't want to play because he was so tired. **e)** Most of the fans bought tickets although they were very expensive. **f)** The performance had already lasted for an hour but the crowd demanded more songs. **g)** After the crowd had asked for another song, the band began to play. **h)** The crowd pushed forward although the police prevented them from getting through.

9. **a)** Malta is a small island in the south of Europe. **b)** The Tower and Buckingham Palace are sights in London. **c)** Eton is an old public school in England. **d)** Autumn is the season between summer and winter. **e)** Your birthday is the day of the year when you were born. **f)** An airport is a place where aeroplanes land or take off. **g)** A musician composes music or plays a musical instrument. **h)** A boarding-school is a school where pupils live.

10. **a)** The White House is the official residence of the US president in Washington. **b)** A cruise liner is a large and comfortable ship with swimming pools and hundreds of waiters. You get plenty of food and drink there. **c)** Lifeboats must be on large ships to rescue passengers when the ship is in danger of sinking. **d)** Commercials are advertisements on radio and television. **e)** A holiday is the time when we have no school. **f)** A crowd is a large number of people joined together in a place. **g)** Breakfast is the first meal in the morning. **h)** Denmark is a small country in Northern Europe. **i)** A donkey is an animal with long ears which looks like a small horse. **j)** A film library is a place where you can borrow films.

11. **a)** … is a sum of money you owe someone / which you have to pay back. **b)** … is someone who knows a lot in a special field. **c)** … was a prehistoric animal. **d)** … is a very high building. In Manhattan, there are a lot of skyscrapers. **e)** … breaks into houses and steals things. **f)** … is a woman who does the cooking, cleaning and shopping for her family. **g)** … is a person who is very interested in computers. **h)** … is a person who is responsible for running a firm.

12. **a)** The disaster happened 400 miles south of Newfoundland at 11.37 p.m. **b)** They believed that the Titanic was unsinkable because of the 16 watertight compartments. **c)** The captain should not have ignored the seven warnings. **d)** There was a strange noise.

Additional Question

I think they want to have a luxury holiday. They can visit different places and needn't drive their own car. (+1) They can leave one place in the evening and be somewhere else in the morning.

13. … You won't believe it, but I'm in Australia. We arrived in Sydney five weeks ago. It seemed awfully hot there since we had left Frankfurt in cold and rainy weather. Then we went to the outback to visit Australia's sight Ayers Rock. It was spectacular. The climate was dry and even hotter than in Sydney. Our accommodation was quite simple. We lived in tents and cooked our meals together. The food was okay although we very often had to live on tinned food. You can't find many supermarkets in Australia's outback. Anyway, we had a wonderful time and met many interesting people. I was very fascinated to learn about Australia's native people who are called Aborigines. There are special programmes to teach Aboriginal children about their own culture. A great idea, isn't it? How about your holiday?

14. He likes doing sports especially team games like handball. But he is also interested in computer games and internet surfing. Apart from this, he likes to meet his friends at weekends. He enjoys school though not every subject. It depends on the teacher. Above all he prefers sciences but does fairly well in languages, too. He likes his parents but he doesn't spend much time with them. They have to work long hours and at the weekends, he is often not at home. As far as his teachers are concerned, it is very different. Some are really boring others give interesting lessons you can profit from even outside school. He quite often goes to handball matches with his friends. As he is a computer fan, he also likes to talk a lot about bytes and bits. Once a week he practises with his handball team. He is not very interested in politics but he is, however, informed about current events and political parties. He is not really pessimistic about the future although he recognises the threat of unemployment. Nobody knows how things will develop, so it is no use being too frightened.

15. a) last Saturday ➧ Last Saturday Bob met his girlfriend Sarah at the cinema.
b) … the police the accident ➧ Tony reported the accident to the police.
d) … on television a film ➧ Yesterday I saw a film on television.
e) … the stick his master ➧ The dog brings his master the stick.